ROME AND CANTERBURY

THE ELUSIVE SEARCH
FOR UNITY

MARY REATH ROME &
CANTERBURY
THE ELUSIVE SEARCH
FOR UNITY

SHEED & WARD
New York · 2007

CONTENTS

FOREWORD – THREE VOICES

THE REV. DR. JOHN MACQUARRIE

> Dr. Macquarrie was Lady Margaret Professor of Divinity in the University of Oxford and Canon Residentiary of Christ Church, Oxford from 1970 until 1986. He is a scholar of Martin Heidegger and is perhaps best known for *Principles of Christian Theology*, a work of systematic theology that aims to harmonize existentialism and orthodox Christianity.

Christianity has now a history of more than two thousand years. In that long time, it has sometimes been advancing, sometimes it has been retreating. At present, it seems to have come to a kind of standstill, especially in Europe and North America. It no longer has the dominance and leadership that it once had among the population of those continents, but it still has plenty of life. But that life is within the church, and not even in all of the church, while in society at large, Christianity is observed, so it would seem, by many people as out of date in the modern scientific world. There are, of course, other parts of the world where Christianity is still a novelty and has a voice in the lives and aspirations of the people.

Looking back on its two thousand years of history, we see a long period of expansion. It seemed possible that Christianity was on the way to becoming a worldwide religion, embodying a high destiny for the whole human race. Century after century, it covered wide areas and held out hopes of an ever more highly developed and spiritually profound human race. But in course of time, that model has come to an end. The Christian powers themselves have fallen short of the ideals of the faith. Churches are reducing rather than expanding their work. What is the future?

I do not think we should be pessimistic in thinking about the future of the Church, but I do think we have got to make profound changes in the way that we consider the Church in relation to the whole human race. Further, I believe this period of change is already beginning to take place. The trouble was beginning in the Middle Ages, when to some extent the Church had become or had sought to become a material power rather than a spiritual power. The Reformation was, to some extent, a revolt against materialism and an attempt to establish the essential spirituality of the church, but it failed and produced in the end only a broken church. On the one hand was the traditional Church in which one had nevertheless to acknowledge a division between the great eastern and western churches and, on the other hand, the multitude of new churches or new pretended churches, growing from the sixteenth century onward into a multitude of sects, most of which could be criticized as only partially Christian, and which were often in complete disagreement, even violent hostility in their relations with one another.

Then something like a miracle began to manifest itself. The so-called ecumenical movement was born. The many relatively small Christian groups began to seek unity among themselves, and this is possible only in an atmosphere of love and purgation.

There is a very long and difficult way to go, and much of it lies still ahead of us. The Protestant bodies will have to find the way to Rome and Rome will have to find an acceptable way of accepting them and whatever may have been valid in the character of each. Overarching these divisions of the west, attention must be given also to the difference between east and west.

Impossible, do we say? I don't think so, but it will need enormous patience, for which we should all be praying. The prayer itself produces the way to the recovery.

The Ecumenical Movement of the present period is drawing us toward this great goal of a church that will be both one, yet catering for the diversities of the human race. No doubt there will be some mistakes, but surely the end, a church united in love and service, can inspire all Christians in their several positions. The ecumenists, sometimes at considerable sacrifice, are showing the way toward a great Christian future. Among them, we gratefully recognize the lovely and hopeful efforts of Mary Reath, and pray that we are brought nearer to the days of full Christian unity.

THE MOST REV. DR. JOHN A BATHERSBY

Archbishop Bathersby is the Roman Catholic Archbishop of Brisbane and the Co-chair of the International Anglican Roman Catholic Commission on Unity and Mission (IARCCUM)

It is a truism to say we live in times of change. This change is more apparent to older people than younger people. Nevertheless within this culture of change, the churches' search for unity moves quite slowly. It is often challenged by the complexity of finding truth in a post-modern world. In today's culture, attempts to stay in communion with one another whether at an international or provincial level is by no means easy. It is within such a context that Anglicans and Roman Catholics seek agreement today.

The spirit-filled Anglican-Roman Catholic meeting in Mississauga, Canada, in 2000, largely between Bishops, finished full of hope. A new body, the International Anglican – Roman Catholic Commission for Unity and Mission (IARCCUM), quickly came into existence and enthusiastically set to work to develop a common statement of agreement and to suggest strategies for ever closer cooperation. The work of the new Commission slowed when the churches of the Anglican Communion entered into a period of dispute concerning matters of human sexuality, and more importantly the nature of the relationship between Anglican provinces. This led to the standing down in 2003 of IARCCUM for approximately a year. The Anglican Communion responded to its internal crisis by establishing a committee under the chairmanship of Archbishop Robin Eames to prepare a text, the Windsor Report (October, 2004), which has served as a blueprint for a possible way forward. The Windsor Report and its suggestions are being studied and assessed in the Anglican provinces, in a process leading up to the Lambeth Conference in 2008.

In the meantime IARCCUM has continued its work, and the recently released Statement "Growing Together in Unity and Mission", without overlooking points of disagreement, is filled with an optimism that is contagious. Paragraph 7 of the introduction states "... it must be acknowledged that the progress towards agreement in faith achieved through the theological dialogue has been substantial, but that in the past four decades we have only just begun to give tangible expression to the incontrovertible elements of shared faith."

The great strength of our relationship resides in the goodwill that straddles the boundaries of our disagreements. This goodwill remains at an international, national, and local level despite present challenges. Moreover it is accompanied by a definite desire to maintain and strengthen our relationship lest it slip back into the unacceptable divisions of the recent past. Mary Reath's fine book will only serve to strengthen this desire in both communions.

THE MOST REV. DR. PETER CARNLEY OA

Archbishop Carnley is the Co-Chair of the Anglican Roman Catholic International Commission (ARCIC), the Chairman of the Archbishop of Canterbury's Panel of Reference and the retired Anglican Archbishop of Australia

The late Pope John Paul II often used to comment that the ecumenical journey is an arduous enterprise. Certainly, those of us who have been involved in the modern Anglican-Roman Catholic dialogue know from hard experience just how much time and effort has to be put into producing an agreed theological statement, or into formulating some practical initiative that the two Churches might together put in place in the painstaking, step by step, process towards the re-establishment of 'full visible unity'. The most recent agreed statement of ARCIC II, for example, 'Mary: Grace and Hope in Christ' (2004) was the result of five years of regular discussion and scholarly debate and countless revisions of proposed texts.

The ecumenical journey is made even more difficult because the 'goal posts are always moving'. No sooner do we think that we have reached a significant level of agreement, than we find a new issue popping up to challenge and frustrate us.

Perhaps, after 400 years of separation we would be foolish to think that the reintegration of the Churches might be easy.

Nevertheless, despite these occasional hiccups along the way, when we see the story 'whole' it becomes increasingly clear that in our day progress towards Christian unity has been a most enormous achievement.

That is why Mary Reath's book is so important. It gives us an eminently readable and readily accessible account of the disintegration of the Church at the time of the 16th Century Reformation and then rehearses the gradual movement towards the re-integration of the Churches in our own time.

To know the story of 'how we got this way' and what has happened in the good purposes of God over the last 40 years cannot fail to inspire and energize us. To have such a well-researched, balanced and lucid account of the journey towards the coming great Church of the future is a blessing in itself: it is an invitation to 'get on board' for what we may justifiably hope may be the final phase of the ecumenical journey. In the context of today's divided and terror ridden world what could be more important for the ultimate well-being of all humanity?

AUTHOR'S NOTE

I had an emotional jolt during a course I took at the Anglican Centre in Rome in 1998. The class, called *Continuity and Change*, educated people from around the worldwide Anglican Communion about the close relationships that exist and that are being re-built between Anglicans/Episcopalians and Roman Catholics, and about how rooted all Western Christian churches are in ancient Rome.

The class was spiritually and intellectually thrilling, with insider tours of Roman and Vatican sites and a trip to Subiaco, where St. Benedict lived in his cave early in the 6th century. We went into the Vatican for a crash course on the workings of the *Curia*, its rather mysterious administrative arm. Another day there was Mass down in the dank *Catacomb of San Callista* and then, on the very next day, we had front row, guest of honor seats for a jubilant papal Eucharist celebrated under the baldacchino at the high altar in St. Peter's. Throughout the ten days, in classes and cafes, we discussed the developed nuances of Roman Catholic and Anglican/Episcopalian teachings on theology and morals.

I was fascinated and, more accurately, stunned to learn that the divisions in Christianity were seen not as a given, but just the opposite rather. The church's redeeming message of love and hope for all is compromised, when it is itself divided. Furthermore, that there were and are determined high level talks working to rebuild relations and to bring the churches back together. Some that are even having some success.

Michael Ramsey, the 100th Archbishop of Canterbury, visited Rome in 1966. It was just after Vatican II, the worldwide meeting of the bishops of the Roman Catholic Church, and he and Pope Paul VI were keenly interested in doing whatever they could to promote reunion between the Roman Catholic and Anglican churches. Together they set in motion the dialogue that would come to be called the Anglican-Roman Catholic International Commission (*ARCIC*), which has been meeting annually since 1970. And shortly afterwards the Anglican Centre was opened in Rome so that both churches could get to know each other better.

I came home craving to understand more about what it was that really separated these two prominent and influential worldwide churches. I mistakenly thought that I could read something that would efficiently summarize the doctrinal differences and that would be that. To the contrary, the story cannot fit into explanatory boxes or a neat graph; it is more akin to a beautiful mathematical theorem or to a complex and grand opera.

The number of scholarly books written with opinions and interpretations on the original breach, on evolving doctrinal and ecclesiological differences, and on everything in-between is huge. But, there isn't much written for lay people, and certainly nothing that covers this search for unity from the historical, doctrinal and practical angles.

We can see that the world's religions are in flux. That they are struggling internally should not surprise us, as the whole world is coming to grips with fundamental changes in how we communicate and how we relate globally. There is great uncertainty about the most effective and authentic ways to lead, and honest confusion about claims of religious truth in our pluralistic age. But the work that has been done to rebuild relations is honestly exciting and will bear fruit. At some future, unknown moment, when the time is right, we'll look around us and be surprised to see a new church, one that we cannot now predict.

When Germans awoke on November 9, 1989, they'd been dreaming that their children might one day walk through the Brandenburg Gate, little knowing that they themselves would do it that afternoon.

Cardinal Walter Kasper, President of the Pontifical Council for Promoting Christian Unity, at the Center for Theological Inquiry, Princeton, November 19, 2002

PREFACE

J ust as I was finishing this book, in the summer of 2006, two events, within weeks of each other and thousands of miles apart, set its ideas and the forty years of dialogue into a new context. On June 18, the Episcopal Church in the US elected a woman, Katharine Jefferts Schori, to lead them and represent them at global meetings of the Anglican Communion. Just weeks later, on July 8, the equivalent body in England, gave the theological go-ahead to prepare for allowing female clergy in England to become bishops.

These two events and their implications have brought to a head discontent that had been simmering for years, and mark a new phase for the Anglican Communion, its leaders and members, and their dialogue partners. These decisions have set it on a very public path toward a possible dissolving of the Anglican Communion as it is today, or of a movement toward a new way, likely using some type of covenant, to experience and manage itself as a worldwide church.

While these developments are a sharp challenge, and with hindsight, not really surprising, this book is the story, of a parallel movement, one that is little known and that will mature and become more interesting as time passes. Following and understanding it is a view into unresolved questions about the relationship between religion and the individual, between religion and the culture, and between autonomy and authority.

As I have said, when I ran across this work, this no-going-back approach to dialogue, it caught me up short. I recognized it as a positive, astonishing, and enormous idea that I think is at the front end of a culture shift.

So this is the story of the determined but little known work being done to end the nearly five hundred year old divisions between the Roman Catholic and the Anglican/Episcopal Churches. The break was never intended, has never been fully accepted and is experienced as a painful and open wound.

That 99 out of 100 people in the United States assume that the general partitions in Christianity are a given, and know nothing about this reunion effort, belies the seriousness with which this is taken at the very top levels of these two churches. Most Americans have no idea of the work and actual progress that the Ecumenical Movement and the search for Christian unity have made and how it might affect their lives someday. They take the conventional divisions in Christianity as a given without understanding that the churches, in spite of very different ways of being perceived by the world, are totally committed to dialogue and see ecumenism as preparing the way for a visionary, still unforeseeable day when they will work together and even be united in some new way.

The church cannot legitimately represent Christ's redeeming message of love and hope when it is not working to heal its own divisions. Indeed, if the church is to thrive and to genuinely serve the poor *and* the poor in spirit, Christian reunion must be the church's highest imperative. Indeed, it is my belief that ecumenical work holds the key to a revitalized Christianity.

I could have chosen any one of the over 100 current theological dialogues to write about – the Anglican-Methodist, the Orthodox-Lutheran, or the Roman Catholic-Pentecostal – to name but three. But I've picked the Anglican-Roman Catholic corner to shine a light into for a couple of reasons. From the beginning, there have been high hopes that this particular dialogue might bear fruit. While vastly smaller than the Roman Catholic Church, the Anglican Communion is also an international body with a distinctively sacramental tradition, that is based on the priority of the Bible vis a vis doctrinal questions, a Book of Common Prayer, and a threefold ministry of bishops, priest and deacons. And secondly, because I was raised in the Roman Catholic Church but have spent twenty-five years of my adult life in the Episcopal Church, the status quo is not tolerable to me. I waver, and wander back and forth between the two churches, alive to the visceral power that I experience in each. I've become intolerably located in both.

The *Anglican-Roman Catholic International Commission (ARCIC)* got underway in 1970. The brief given to them by Pope Paul VI and Archbishop of Canterbury Michael Ramsey was "a serious dialogue which, founded on the Gospels and on the ancient common traditions, may lead to that unity in truth, for which Christ prayed." Their specialized theological mandate has set them out of the mainstream, but they have produced nine remarkable documents that demonstrate much agreement and convergence.

I often see a 'fight or flight' response begin to build when I speak about this subject and these ideas. Division, after all, has defined Christian identity for generations, and imagining any type of change, let alone reunion, sounds unbelievable and for many just plain undesirable. Deep questions and strong feelings are stirred.

These two particular churches seem to symbolize such different ways of operating, but the story is more complicated. Churches are actually living cultures with teachings and practices that do evolve. There should be no assumptions that what are seen currently as stumbling blocks will remain in place forever, that there isn't some "yet to be imagined" new relationship. Neither church wants to give up the theological progess that's been made and the friendships that have been rebuilt.

I'm not trying to lighten the genuine problems or to diminish identity, but rather to slow down our immediate assumptions and introduce some different ways of thinking about the churches and their relationships with each other. Unspoken historical perceptions, particularly about the pope, and sometimes fanned by the popular media, are inaccurate and de-stabilizing.

Archbishop of Canterbury Rowan Williams said on June 11, 2003,

> Once we are clearer about the nature and scope of religious disagreement, we are actually more rather than less likely to develop a respectful and collaborative practice in inter-faith relations.

The situation is similar within the different branches of Christianity. Religion for most of us is like politics. It is local, which means that it is experiential. We can't imagine what difference some type of reunion might actually look like or feel like in our own churches or what difference it would make at the international level, but in the end this is one theology, with rich and parallel interpretations, talking about their joint ancestors, and realizing that they are actually one family, united by baptism into a type of communion that really already exists.

*

We have worshipped without knowledge of this endeavor, and when we learn about it, it's tempting to say that it still doesn't have anything to do with us. But it is past time for these ideas to be more broadly known, because reunion could never come solely or even primarily from above; a paper reunion would be meaningless. In the end, without the laity involved, this will never happen.

Embittered relations have run their course, especially in today's world of ever more intricate communication and networks. The relationships that have been and are being rebuilt across the leadership of the world's huge international churches are an aid and resource for our new century and its affairs.

This is not a political accommodation; nor is it a short term project. This is a big, new paradigm-shifting idea for a world in need of hope. Thoughtful readers will be surprised to learn about this no-going-back new day.

I believe what my friend Peggy Laughlin wrote me,

> When it finally occurs the whole world will be affected and life will be different.

CHAPTER ONE

THE BREACH IN THE WEST

It may seem unnecessary to begin at the Reformation, and it certainly slows this story down, but if we are to begin to imagine a different future world, we must go back and begin when Western Christianity divided. It is also a good idea because it it is likely that there are misconceptions about what motivated Henry VIII and Martin Luther in the early years of the 16th century. Certainly when they started, two such fervent Catholics never desired that their lives and actions would initiate the break-up of Western Christendom, thereby altering people's fundamental experience of the Christian religion.

The huge transformations that they unintentionally set in motion would never have taken root if the times hadn't been so peculiarly ripe for change. It would be almost impossible to over-state the extent to which their actions were empowered by the powerful new tool of the printing press and by the recent Renaissance ideas of the uniqueness of each and every person. At this moment of radical change, the actions of these men were about to re-shape the truths on which people's beliefs had been based for hundreds of years.

Lives in the early 1500's were still centered around small and contained units of family, work and church, but the explorations and discoveries of Columbus (1492) and daGama (1497), and Magellan's circumnavigation of the world (1517-1522) meant that small cities, and soon local villages and towns, were being exposed to unfamiliar ideas. People's deep-seated assumptions about the centrality of their history or of being unique in the world were being questioned. They were used to monarchs and popes trading dominance, and power and land being redistributed from time to time, but the printing press, world exploration and new Renaissance ideas about the individuality of each person inaugurated something altogether different.

Religious movements cannot be seen in isolation, and the Protestant Reformation was the natural playing out of a long, slow, culture-wide fermentation. The time was ripe for elementary changes in Christian order.

History names Martin Luther and Henry VIII as two of the instigators of the break-up of Western Christendom. Their individual and unique contributions to the events shaped it, but they had merely ignited a latent spark, and then found themselves swept along by something greater, and other, than they had intended or envisioned.

MARTIN LUTHER

Catholic priest and Augustinian friar Martin Luther was a teaching theologian in Wittenberg, in central Germany, in 1517, when his anxious conscience got in the way of the private practice of his faith. He was a young man, 33 years old, and he agonized over his personal weaknesses, and over the fallen state of humanity. Most especially he had a private fear: he worried that he was primarily afraid of hell, and not *really* adequately sorry for his sins.

Pope Leo X, and Pope Julius II before him, were raising money for the rebuilding of St. Peter's in Rome, and began to do so by selling indulgences, which were purchased documents that reduced the amount of time the purchaser had to spend in purgatory, atoning for his sins, and thereby purchasing forgiveness for those sins. This was the final straw for the scrupulous Luther.

It is odd for us today to try to grasp the rationality and conventionality of indulgences, but in Luther's time, they were popular with the people and with the church hierarchy. They were introduced in the late 1200's, at about the same time that paper money was beginning to replace the barter system, and were quite a logical product of the period. They offered people two important benefits.

Firstly, by purchasing an indulgence, the faithful helped the church, which had a legitimate need for large sums of money since it and not the state, was the provider of social services. Secondly, the purchaser was also buying something safer than a lottery ticket. It was a spiritual life insurance policy that might help him, or a relative, to avoid punishment in the afterlife. The buyer held a physical piece of paper, which provided tangible proof that he or she had purchased the use of the prior accumulated (leftover) goodness of others. A purchased indulgence did not absolve the sin itself, but it was a buy-out of the punishment, perhaps somewhat analogous to buying air rights for development or emissions rights today.

Later, spurred on by their popularity and his printing press's ability to print large quantities of them, Gutenberg himself printed upwards of 200,000 indulgences.*

*Alister McGrath, *In The Beginning*, p. 18

One of Gutenberg's Indulgences of 1454–5

In his *95 Theses*, which Luther posted on the door of the Catholic Schlosskirche, in Wittenberg, on October 31, 1517, he seeringly denounced the practice of indulgences. As Owen Chadwick says,

> ...indulgences made a lot of money for good causes and some less good, and they were part of people's piety; so they were defended. But no one could defend them by saying it is a reasonable act to buy forgiveness, or by claiming they were taught in the Bible. The only defense possible was that the pope authorized them; therefore Friar Martin [Luther] was a heretic because he denied the authority of the pope. And Friar Martin of the whirling pen had an easy answer. Buying forgiveness is obviously

wrong. If the pope authorizes it, the pope is wrong. It cannot be heresy to say what is true.

Owen Chadwick, *History of Christianity,* p. 202

The pope sent Cardinal Cajetan (Thomas de Vio), a skilled diplomat, to Germany to challenge Luther's thinking. Their exchange only served to encourage Luther to clarify with even more rigor, his ideas about sin, to which he soon added his concerns about the papal abuses of power.

For Luther, each unique individual's personal faith and belief in Jesus Christ carried integrity and an intensity that was more vital than any man-made institution or interlocutor. He had studied and struggled with the ideas of Augustine and the church fathers, and didn't believe that any had it quite right. He believed that people desired to be good in order to achieve salvation, but he also understood the difficulty that people have in really *believing* that they were living good lives and therefore deserving of God's freely given grace. He thought that personal weakness and fallenness and an inability to feel God's grace were dominant in the human condition.

Luther didn't have a problem with the teachings of the Catholic Church, or even with the way it governed itself. His complaint was that too many people in the organization had become corrupt, that false teachings about indulgences were leading ordinary lay people astray and that its legalistic ideas of guilt and merit were not helpful to people.

> Luther struggled to become right with God by the observance of law and by the penitential practice bound up with the later medieval doctrine of grace and human merit. He wrestled for a forgiveness and a union with God which was regarded as in part God's gift but in part something earned by a man's own practice of virtue. As with St. Paul, Luther's sensitiveness to the moral meaning of God's righteousness and his awareness of the entire incapacity of man to possess merit before God led him to the agony of despair over what the law could not do.*

*A. M. Ramsey, *The Gospel and the Catholic Church,* p. 182

Charles V, the last of the Holy Roman Emperors, and emperor from 1519-1558, dominated Europe, controlling Spain, Naples, Spanish America and the Low Countries. He knew that his empire required a united Christendom, and he thought that the pope, Leo X, needed to do something about the trouble and excitement that Luther was generating. An assembly of the Holy Roman Empire, the 1521 *Diet of Worms*, was coming up, which Charles would lead, and Leo and Charles planned to have Luther condemned.

But they miscalculated. Luther was such a powerful thinker and speaker that his words made a deep impression. Only after he had departed, were they able to impose sanctions against him. A papal bull formally excommunicated Luther in the same year.

Charles was preoccupied with the Moslem Turkish army that was threatening Vienna, which was attacked in 1529, and that in 1534 "raided at will along the coasts of Sicily and Naples, then seized Tunis, in North Africa as a base for further operations."* These incursions kept

*James D. Tracy, *Europe's Reformations, 1450-1650*, p. 138

LIFE AND TIMES OF CHARLES V (1500 – 1558)
Last of the Holy Roman Emperors

Charles V was at the center of the inter-related powers and events in an age of great change: global exploration and discovery, the invention of the printing press, the break-up of Western Christianity, and the growth of Islam.

His family

His grandparents were Ferdinand and Isabella who sent Christopher Columbus.

His mother was Joanna, one of their daughters.

His mother's sister was Catharine of Aragon (1485-1536) who married Henry VII and then his brother, Henry VIII.

His son married Mary, daughter of his aunt Catherine and Henry VIII.

His explorers

Sent Magellan around the world (1517-1522).

Extended his lands through discoveries of Cortes and Pizarro.

His political control

Parts of Spain, Ghent, the Low Countries, and Burgundy.

His wars

Sacked Rome in 1527 to intimidate Henry VIII, imprisoned Pope Clement VII

Fought Francis I (France) with support from Henry VIII

Fought Sultan Sulieman and his armies repeatedly, winning victories in Vienna (1529) and Tunis (1535)

His religious control

Called for and went to the Diet of Worms in 1521 to sanction Luther

Supported the Council of Trent

---

him from paying adequate attention to the problems that were being caused by Luther in Charles's German territories. Indeed, successful Muslim incursions in Hungary, Spain and Cyprus made it an especially volatile and precarious time for Christianity. Survival was a serious concern and legitimate fear for Christianity, especially because the number of Muslim converts was growing, and worldwide, there were actually more Muslims than Christians in this period.

Martin Luther's beliefs were especially influenced by the ideas of Erasmus (1466-1536), a scholar and critic of some church habits and teachings. Erasmus advocated reform, but believed that it should come from within the Catholic Church. When he was accused of having laid the egg that Luther hatched, "he half admitted the charge, but said he had expected quite another bird." (Owen Chadwick, *History of Christianity*, p. 202)

Luther's treatise *The Freedom of a Christian* (1520) makes clear his conviction, arrived at after anguishing doubt, that salvation comes by saying 'yes' to God's grace, which is given freely to all, and is not dependent on anyone's good works or on any earthly authority - particularly not on any salvation via an indulgence that could be purchased. Man's sinfulness is a given and salvation comes purely and solely from God's grace and his love for his creation, not from good works, personal piety, church membership or purchased indulgences. Like St. Paul, Luther believed any individual is justified in the eyes of God not by what he does in this world, but by his faith, by his inner desire to receive God's freely given grace and love, which Luther also defined as a 'work.'

This affair of the conscience set in motion an unstoppable flow of events that unintentionally led to the break-up of Latin Christendom.

It wasn't until almost 500 years later, on November 31, 1999, after discussing these matters for 34 years, that the Roman Catholic Church and the Lutheran World Federation, were able to come to a common formulation on how we are saved.

In the words of the document,

We can confess together: By grace alone, in faith in Christ's saving work and not because of any merit on our part, we are accepted by God and receive the Holy Spirit, who renews our hearts while equipping and calling us to good works. (No. 15)

This *Joint Declaration on the Doctrine of Justification* did not completely settle all questions and nuances regarding the two Churches' teachings about justification. Nonetheless, it was an extraordinary breakthrough, proving that what had once seemed impossible had been accomplished.

The Joint Declaration was signed by Cardinal Cassidy, President of the *Pontifical Council for Promoting Christian Unity*, and the Reverend Dr. Ishmael Noko, General Secretary of the *World Lutheran Federation.*

Since then, there has been a strong move for the member churches of the World Methodist Council to also affirm the common statements of the Joint Declaration.

HENRY VIII

Henry VIII would surely be shocked to learn that his actions had contributed to a break in Christianity that has lasted to the present day. He had no quarrel with Catholic doctrine and venerated the Blessed Sacrament daily. What was essentially a jurisdictional dispute in his day has now become a doctrinal one.

When Luther's ideas and those of other reformers circulated in England, Henry VIII vigorously refuted them in a book about the sacraments, for which Pope Leo X (in 1521) gave him the title *Defender of the Faith,* and Henry had had all of Luther's books banned by 1530. An amateur theologian, Henry VIII was faithful to the doctrines of the Catholic Church, believing that the theologies of Luther, John Calvin and other reformers to be heretical. He also opposed all calls from Rome for an ecumenical council to discuss the religious upheaval that was going on in northern Europe.

Henry died believing he was a good and faithful Catholic, and that the friction with Rome would not last. In a speech to Parliament in 1545, he made a call for Christian unity based on St. Paul's first letter to the Corinthians, Chapter 13.

> If I speak in the tongues of men and of angels, but do not have love, I am a noisy gong or a clanging cymbal. And if I have prophetic powers, and understand all mysteries, and knowledge, and if I have all faith, so as to move mountains, but do not have love, I am nothing. (*I Corinthians 13:1-2*)

Henry's quest and the eventual forming of the Church of England, called Anglican in much of the world today, and Episcopalian in the United States, was driven by one thing and one thing only: his utter determination to carry out his one essential responsibility as king. His marrying six women was a sensationally desperate, and, to state it kindly, extreme attempt to perform his most fundamental duty as monarch – to produce an heir, most particularly a male heir. Yes, there was church property that he stood to gain, but he was primarily asserting the normal rights of a sovereign of his day. It is hard for us to imagine a time when a pope's secular and religious power was so great.

The fact that he had needed a papal dispensation to marry Catherine in the first place unsettled him. When Catherine's four male babies died in infancy and only one daughter survived, he was in despair.

> For a king to have but one legitimate heir was worry enough; for that heir to be female was, given patriarchal and feudal concepts of competence and authority, a national nightmare.
>
> Christopher Haigh, *English Reformations*, p. 89

Henry's father, Henry VII, had required Pope Julian II's dispensation to initiate Henry's first marriage. It was against church rules for him to marry Catherine of Aragon, since she was his brother's widow and they thereby had a 'contracted affinity,' meaning a prior legal relationship. She was the daughter of Queen Isabella and King Ferdinand of Spain, and importantly, aunt to the previously mentioned Charles V, Europe's most powerful monarch, the man whom Pope Leo X had sent to the Diet of Worms to silence Luther. Henry was only eleven years old when he was betrothed to the seventeen-year old Catherine.

This was the quintessential arranged marriage. The fathers, Ferdinand and Henry VII, needed each other to keep France quieted and the alignment was finally solidified when the marriage took place in June of 1509. Henry was 18, and Catherine 24.

Around this time common-law marriages, which had been the norm for most people, were beginning to be regularized with witnesses, and the blessing of a priest. This was thought to be beneficial, especially if the couple wanted children.* But arranged marriages, sometimes established at birth, were the norm for the wealthy and for dynastic monarchies, serving to solidify alliances and reorganize territory.

* Chadwick, *History of Christianity*, p. 155-156

These arranged marriages did not originate as love-matches, so adultery was not unusual, and since, on occasion, alliances needed to be changed, divorces and annulments existed. These divorces and annulments were granted fairly routinely, often on grounds that were invented to be expedient. These quasi-trumped-up reasons often related to distant blood relationships or to former contracted affinities, which could then be used later to invalidate the wedding.

After nearly twenty years of what is described as a happy marriage with Catherine, Henry began to fear that the lack of a male heir was divine retribution for his having married his brother's widow, something clearly forbidden in the Bible, and, Henry now believed, offensive to God. After all, Catherine had given birth to four sons each of whom had lived for only a few weeks. She had also given birth to a daughter, Mary, born in 1516, who survived. Henry determined that his duty required him to marry someone who could produce a male heir. He needed an annulment.

He fully expected that his divorce, really an annulment, from Catherine would be granted because it usually was for someone in his position. His two sisters, Mary Tudor and Margaret, widow of James IV of Scotland, had each had annulments; King John of England, King Louis XII of France, and the Emperor Maximilian I, grandfather to Charles V and father-in-law to Henry's wife, and Catherine's sister also had each had annulments.*

*Bernard and Margaret Pawley, *Rome and Canterbury Through Four Centuries*, p. 5

Pope Clement VII was not opposed to granting Henry's divorce, but he was balancing delicate and competing demands. Catherine's nephew, Charles V, was more powerful than Henry VIII and he attacked Rome for seven months in 1527. Pope Clement got the message. He could neither ignore Charles, nor the honor of Charles' aunt Catherine, Henry's wife. There would be no annulment for Henry.

> As the grandson of Ferdinand and Isabella and the nephew of Catherine, Charles was intent that neither pope nor English king would set aside the royal daughter of Spain. He was also vitally concerned that an annulment would remove Henry and Catherine's one child, his cousin Mary Tudor, from succession to the throne of England. And that could rob Spain of the opportunity to influence the affairs of England.*

* David L. Holmes, *A Brief History of the Episcopal Church,* p. 192

At the same time, Henry sought to further consolidate his power, and to limit the power of the pope in England, and that of the English bishops, monks and clergy. He desperately did *not* want to break with Rome, and the requisite need for an heir, propelled Henry and his emissaries to seek the annulment intensely, and they began a public relations campaign with Roman diplomats.

Lawyers and theologians, including rabbinical scholars, were consulted, and the royal divorce was debated internationally. Henry was frantic. Extensive documents were drafted in order to prove that his marriage to Catherine was not lawful and should never have been allowed in the first place, on the legitimate and conventional grounds that she was his brother's widow.

By the middle of 1529, university opinions in favor of an annulment had been obtained from Paris, Orleans, Bologna, Padua, and three others. But Angers had declared against Henry, the pope had silenced Perugia, the Venetian civil authorities had forbidden discussion; elsewhere Charles V's bribes were bigger than Henry's. It was a helpful, but not very impressive collection, and certainly not the academic consensus that might have induced the pope to change his mind.

> It seems clear that judgments on the Aragon marriage as yet bore no relationship to any emerging divisions between Catholics and Protestants, in England or in Europe. Since there seemed no prospect that the issue would be solved except within the framework of papal law and theology, it had no broader implications.
>
> Christopher Haigh, *English Reformations,* p. 100-1

Interestingly, Martin Luther saw no reason that Henry VIII should be granted an annulment on the grounds that he claimed, and opposed it. Eventually Henry's case rested on the claim that his annulment was vital to England's national interest.

> For by September, 1530 Henry's divorce think-tank had produced just what the king needed: a collection of documents and precedents used to show that the English Church had provincial rights and independent jurisdiction, and that the English king had sovereign authority over Church and realm. . . . at the end of August 1530 Henry instructed his ambassadors at Rome to tell the pope that by ancient privilege no English-man could be cited outside the realm to answer to a foreign jurisdiction
>
> Christopher Haigh, *English Reformations*, p. 102

Henry's strategy had evolved over years and in the end, its success depended on having the English clergy agree that the king's word held sway in his own realm. He successfully drove a nationalistic and juris-dictional wedge between the English clergy and Rome, and the English Parliament, in 1534, passed the Act of Supremacy, which confirmed to Henry and his successors the title of 'the only supreme head on earth of the Church of England.'

The English bishops' resistance had been worn down, and because they were English after all, they were susceptible to claims of England's final authority over the pope. In Henry's determination to present a male heir, he revivified the idea of a blended imperial and religious authority and initiated the beginnings of something new. He was trying to found a dif-ferent version of Catholicism, one that wasn't tied to Rome.

Thomas Cranmer, the author of the Anglican classic, the *Book of Common Prayer*, issued the annulment in May of 1533. Though Henry did not want to face it, the path was clear. In 1534, he ended papal authori-ty in Britain. Rome had little choice but to excommunicate him, which was done by Pope Paul III, in 1538. In 1539, under Henry's direction, Parliament endorsed a celibate clergy, the doctrine of transubstantia-tion, and confession. Churches were instructed to have a large Bible available for anyone who wished to read it. Though Henry never fully accepted it, the further he and Rome moved toward claims of separate jurisdiction, the closer they moved to a complete break.

The inconceivable religious transformations initiated by Henry VIII did not happen smoothly. The eleven years between his death in 1547 and the beginning of his daughter Elizabeth's reign were violent and bloody. The country reeled under the gyrations of two short and religiously opposed reigns. Edward VI, Henry's son by Jane Seymour, his third wife, and king from Henry's death until 1553, moved the country in a more Protestant direction, but when his sister Mary, the daughter of Catherine of Aragon, assumed power, she reversed direction and restored papal power and the Catholic Church in England.

CHAPTER TWO

A NEW CHRISTIAN LANDSCAPE

PROTESTANT

By the time of Luther's death (1546), there were many churches, not just one, and 'Lutherans' were battling the followers of Geneva's John Calvin, among others, for the loyalty of new converts. Most of the new religious bodies were backed by governments that had armies as well as printing presses to defend their beliefs. Thus religious loyalties now cut across all the others, dividing brother from sister, villager from villager, parishioner from parishioner, guild brother from guild brother. Many Europeans drew spiritual consolation and a more confident view of life from the new religious communities, including the Catholic Church, which found new vigor in facing the Protestant challenge. Others found in the spaces created by open conflict among the contending forms of Christianity greater freedom not to practice any religion at all. Religious rivalry also became a potent additive to the normal stew of political conflict that bred incessant warfare among Europe's many states. Thus the Reformation created a new world in Europe, one recognizably similar in some ways to the pluralistic world that we ourselves inhabit.*

*James D. Tracy, *Europe's Reformations, 1450-1650*, p. 1

Ulrich Zwingli and John Calvin, among a number of other reformers, were inventive and committed believers and doers, whose religious thinking and leadership was now outside the Catholic Church. They were quickly creating the underpinnings for new religious experiences in northern Europe and beyond.

ROMAN CATHOLICISM AND THE COUNTER-REFORMATION

During the 1520's and 30's, the papacy had an inadequate or a conflicted concern for what was going on in northern Europe. The Fifth Lateran Council had only just ended in March of 1517, just seven months before Luther's manifesto. As Norman Tanner has said about the close of the Fifth Lateran Council,

. . . there is an extraordinary lack of awareness of the impending storm.

> The words of the final decree of the council, announcing the closing of the council, are especially disturbing: "Finally, it was reported to us (Pope Leo X) on several occasions, through the cardinals and prelates of the three committees (of the council), that no topics remained for them to discuss and that over several months nothing at all new had been brought before them by anyone."
>
> Norman Tanner, *The Councils of the Church*, p. 74

There were botched Catholic attempts at reform in the mid-1530's, coincidentally opposed by Henry VIII, and stalled by internecine conflict. *Consilium de Emendenda Ecclesia*, a report issued in 1537 that was commissioned to analyze the general situation, centered the blame for Luther's success on papal corruption and on the attitude of the Curia, the inner leadership of the Catholic Church, and on the cardinals. However, disagreements about possible solutions doomed the report.

Still trying to orchestrate a papal approval for his divorce at this time, Henry VIII didn't take Martin Luther very seriously. For him, the English squabble with Rome was just about jurisdiction, not doctrine, and he believed that that it would be resolved without a separation.

Some Catholic leaders advocated reaching out and working more closely with Luther, and others thought his heretical ideas should be stamped out. Both courses were pursued in fits and starts, one side having a dialogue in Germany, and the other establishing a Roman inquisition. Finally, Paul III, pope from 1534 to 1549, began to clean out the worst of the internal corruption and decadence.

A charming and brainy Roman nobleman, and successful papal treasurer, he was made a cardinal deacon when only 25 years old. Though personally he had symbolized the worldly decadence and corruption that was synonymous with Rome and the papacy of that period, he possessed a genuine piety and knew that reform was essential. When he was named the bishop of Parma in 1509, he determined to begin at home. In 1513, he gave up his mistress, by whom he had had four children, and was ordained to the priesthood in 1519.

Ultimately, seeing the Protestant reforming movements as unstoppable and knowing that Roman restructuring was overdue, Pope Paul and the

Catholic hierarchy called for a council, to be held in Trent, in northern Italy. Its fourteen sessions, which began in 1545 and ended in 1563, initiated the process of inner reform, by clarifying church doctrine and renewing discipline.

If Catholic leaders had begun this process when it had been called for earlier, world and religious history would likely be very different. But the unimaginable had become fact, and it had happened very rapidly; western Christianity had broken apart, and a seriously divided church was becoming an irrefutable given.

The council was held in Trent in order to attract German participation, but it was attended primarily by Italian, Spanish and French bishops. There were four English-speaking bishops at Trent, three from England and one from Ireland. With prodding from conservative Spain, the European powerhouse of the 16th century, the Council of Trent changed the order of the church.

The council re-stated church teaching on Scripture, original sin, and the sacraments. In order to raise the moral and professional level of the clergy, new institutions called seminaries were created to train young men. The Council of Trent foreshadowed the issue of infallibility when it stated, "The Church cannot err in delivering Articles of Faith, or Precepts of Morality, inasmuch as it is guided by the Holy Spirit."

The Order of Jesuits had been created in 1540, and at Trent, they pledged themselves as papal missionaries. This initiated a period of worldwide growth for the Roman Catholic Church.

The decisions made at the Council of Trent exhibited a deft mix of religious zeal and political pragmatism. The effect of the reforms was to stabilize church membership, and to formalize the practices of a church that was moving to the newly discovered parts of the world and becoming a worldwide institution.

ANGLICAN

In the end, it was Henry's daughter, Elizabeth I, who piloted a course that ended the religious upheavals and persecutions of the years between her father's death and her crowning. Like her father before her, Elizabeth was excommunicated by Rome, in 1570, the last monarch to be so dealt with. Her early moderate Protestant training, the readiness of the English populace for some religious calm, her clear-eyed sense of her power and her canny political skill created religious peace, and set a climate for her long reign (1558-1603) and for the development and establishment of a native English Church.

Very intentionally, the foundational writings of the newly established Church of England are moderate documents. Thomas Cranmer's earlier *Book of Common Prayer* and the *39 Articles*, approved in 1571, were intended to calm the waters. The *39 Articles* sought to chart a middle way, between Catholic liturgical life and Lutheran reform. They re-articulated the teachings and the beliefs of the first four ecumenical councils, maintained the sacraments and attempted to clarify the contemporary doctrinal confusions about transubstantiation and predestination. Though her thinking was unmistakably independent of Rome, Elizabeth sought to preserve as much of Roman Catholicism as she felt was prudent, and to simultaneously attract new thinkers and ideas, including those of Ulrich Zwingli, Martin Luther and John Calvin.

Her overriding interest had little to do with religion; it was in stabilizing England's place and her power. To that end, and in order to build up a native English church, she suppressed equally both Roman Catholics and Protestants, and she especially shut out the Puritans, who were the English followers of John Calvin. With the passing of the *Acts of Supremacy and Uniformity*, in 1559, she promoted the primacy of temporal authority over sacred authority, which even today gives the British prime minister a say in the naming of the Archbishop of Canterbury and all English diocesan bishops.

She maintained the *39 Articles*, which is as much an historic document as a theological one, as it avoids over-precision in defining the mysteries of the church. Attempting to too finely parse and describe the ineffable, the idea of the holy, would only be divisive.

This document and the *Book of Common Prayer* shaped Anglicanism's moderate ethos, and helped to embed homegrown Anglicanism in a country that blended its established religion with its developing national identity. By the end of Elizabeth's reign in 1603, many Protestant sects had emerged and each was separate, with no status or unity and a building animosity, toward the throne and toward each other.

After her death, religious, constitutional, and economic conflicts combined in an explosive mix that resulted in the English Civil Wars, also called the Puritan Revolution. It took until the mid-1600's for the monarchy, the established church, and parliament to regain their footing, with a broader religious toleration now present.

But the new Anglican Church had been birthed, and its 'via media' route reflected the times in which it came into being and the internal struggle to find a blend of the sacramental life, the majesty and liturgy of Catholicism and of the more 'rooted in the world' emerging Protestant sects.

CHAPTER THREE

ROME AND CANTERBURY FACE MODERNITY

So Christians in the West divided and it took almost 300 years for them to begin to even imagine rethinking their divisions. The lever was 19th century modernism.

In the mid-1800's, the whole Western world was becoming a very different place, as the modern era established its forms. The economy was growing in a rush, due principally to mechanized manufacturing and to the railroads. The first passenger trains began to run in the 1830's, creating the need for, by the 1850's, the international synchronization of time. The growth in wealth was unprecedented in human history.

But, principally, it was the new and seductive scientific ways of thinking that captured imaginations and this began to threaten church order. All ideas and beliefs, even and especially ones about religion, were beginning to be subject to scientific verification. Darwin's theories on the origins of the physical world and on how humans had evolved, published in 1859, and the ideas of the Enlightenment seemed to offer improved alternatives to the habits and activities of the churches, whose reputations had been tarnished by internal excesses and corruption, and internecine wars.

The institutional churches were baffled by these developments and weren't sure how to respond to them. Eventually, the embattled leadership in both Rome and Canterbury called for a more clearly defined church order, with a more centralized and authoritative voice for church leaders.

ROMAN CATHOLIC

The general disestablishment of the Roman Catholic Church in the emerging republican states of the 19th century and the ensuing reorganization hugely changed the identity of each. With developing ideas of individual freedom, responsibilities and rights, the European mood was strongly anti-clerical and anti-church. The need for separate constitutional orders was becoming clear.

The centuries old system of governance that linked secular and church leadership was being re-thought and reformed all over Catholic Europe, and often in turmoil and confusion. There were fears that France would follow Henry VIII's 16th century example and found a national church.

Newly constituted states were coming into being across Europe. The political power of the Roman Catholic Church waned as republics replaced monarchies. More than two dozen concordats between 1801 and 1834 were needed for the church to secure its freedom to even exist in these new countries. Steps to a thoroughly different and modern dance were being invented for the churches.

The temporal power of the papacy was in free-fall, nowhere more so than in Italy. Papal claims to the lands that had been in their control for hundreds of years were unenforceable, and perceived as getting in the way of the desire for a unified Italy. Papal lands were repeatedly invaded, and finally overrun in 1870.

The papacy needed to clarify and establish its temporal base in order to insure its very survival, and quite logically its stances and approaches became more centralized as its temporal power shrank. The personhood of the pope and of his office began to be built up and exalted in a new way. This coincided with the beginnings of the popularization of mass culture and the easy dissemination of images. Pius IX, pope from 1846-1878, was the first pope whose face was known internationally.

The relationship of the papacy to each of these emerging states, and more importantly, to its worldwide network of bishops and priests, was in flux. The following quote shows how dispersed the authority was before disestablishment required greater 'hands-on' and over-sight.

> When Pope Leo XII died in 1829, there were 646 diocesan bishops of the Latin churches. Of these, 555 were appointed by the state; 67 were appointed by Cathedral chapters or the equivalent. Direct appointment of bishops, apart from the Papal States, was confined to 24 dioceses.
>
> John R. Quinn, *The Reform of the Papacy*, p. 122

The era of the assertion of Roman control of all of the worldwide Roman Catholic churches began. As churches were disestablished, bishops and priests from all parts of the world began *for the first time* to be directly appointed by and tied to Roman authority. The dispersed power and the local control of the churches ended, as disestablishment and an embattled Papacy determined that survival required a more powerful centralized authority.

The intellectual basis for some of the ideas about papal centrality were developed by Count Joseph de Maistre in *Du Pape* (1819). His ideas came to be called ultramontanism, which is the belief that the Roman Catholic Church's influence and centralized control should not be limited to Italy, but should extend beyond the Alps (the 'montanes') and throughout the world.

> There can be no public morality and no national character without religion; there can be no Christianity without Catholicism; there can be no Catholicism without the pope; there can be no pope without the sovereignty that belongs to him.
>
> deMaistre in Klaus Schatz,
> *Papal Primacy, From Its Origins to the Present*, p. 148

This reactionary thinking, forged in the fear that supreme monarchs, witness Napoleon, could subvert and control the church and the pope, initiated a fundamental shift in the power that the pope claimed for himself. It created the need for a base that would be centered in his office and with his immediate counselors in the Curia, the Vatican's administrative offices. This was a signal moment in the church's life, one that effectively narrowed the thinking of the whole church, not least because all of the popes and virtually the entire Curia were Italian.

It was in 1846 that Pius IX came in as a youthful, 55 year old modernizing patriot. His predecessor, Gregory XVI, had complained that even Pius's cats were liberal, but that interpretation of his persona didn't last long. Within two years of his installation, there was a violent political push toward the unification of Italy, and Pius was literally forced to take off his papal garb, to disguise himself and to run for his life, as Rome fell into revolution. He received personal encouragement from Queen Victoria in a letter, in January of 1849, but declined her offer of asylum in Malta.

This terrifying assault transformed Pius. He was described as being affable and personally likable, but the attacks on his temporal power and the liberal political scene hardened his thinking, and his leadership began to direct the worldwide church down a narrowing route. His actions and decisions set the shape and tone for a way of thinking, some of which survives in the Roman Catholic Church of today.

Pius IX set a new precedent by, on his own, without calling a council, declaring, in 1854, that the popular, yet controversial, belief that Mary, the mother of Jesus Christ, was born free of original sin and that this was now to be an essential part of Roman Catholic doctrine. His declaration, the bull *Ineffabilis Deus*, says that "from the first moment of her conception the Blessed Virgin Mary was, by the singular grace and privilege of Almighty God, in view of the merits of Jesus Christ, Savior of Mankind, kept free from all stain of original sin."

Ten years later, in 1864, Pius IX issued the *Syllabus of Errors*, a list of 80 anathemas. Most were restatements of existing teachings, but the harsh tone and the timing portrayed an embattled and anti-modern papacy. The way to combat modernity was to claim a direct connection to a godly authority, and to assert a truth that was tied to something not of this world. Declaring truth would make it so. There were moderate Roman Catholic voices that called for searching out what might be the positive aspects of modern thinking, but they were in the minority.

A few of the anathemas went further. Number 77 said that there was no salvation outside of the Church and Number 80 declared "whosoever teaches that the Roman Pontiff ought to reconcile and adjust himself with progress, liberalism, and modern civilization 'let him be anathema.'"* At this embattled moment, Pius IX called for a general council, the first to be called since the Council of Trent in 1545, which had been called to stabilize the church after the Protestant Reformation.

*Bernard and Margaret Pawley, *Rome and Canterbury Through Four Centuries*, p. 210

This was far longer than the church had ever waited to call for a new council. It was the first one to be held in the Vatican, and it began on December 8, 1869, 324 years after the Council of Trent.

The Council was called so the Church could wrestle with what it meant to be a church in this time of new governments without established churches, and to address contemporary ideas in science and the rising rights and freedoms of individuals. Over seven hundred bishops came, representing five continents, though over half were from Italy and France. While Vatican I is best known for defining the dogma of papal infallibility, it also attempted to relate and connect matters of faith to the modern world.

The first decree the council passed was the *Constitution on the Catholic Faith*, and its fourth chapter is called Faith and Reason. In it the church seeks

> to steer a middle course between an excessive exaltation of the authority of reason, exemplified by much of the Enlightenment, on the one hand, and a rejection of reason, often characteristic of religious fundamentalism and a part of the Romantic movement, on the other hand.
>
> Norman Tanner, *The Councils of the Church*, p. 88

Here is an excerpt from the same decree.

> Even though faith is above reason, there can never be any real disagreement between faith and reason, since it is the same God who reveals the mysteries and infuses faith, and who has endowed the human mind with the light of reason . . . Not only can faith and reason never be at odds with one another but they mutually support each other, for on the one hand right reason established the foundations of the faith and, illuminated by its light, develops the science of divine things; on the other hand, faith delivers reason from errors and protects it and furnishes it with knowledge of many kinds.
>
> Norman Tanner, *The Councils of the Church*, p. 89

These modern and reasonable statements don't sound like the set up for a discussion on papal infallibility, nor was the topic initially specifically slated for discussion at Vatican I. However the concept of it had been discussed for years. Most liberal thinkers hoped it would not be raised, for they feared that attempting to declare and define infallibility would only bring distortion to the ideas that lay behind the infallibility concept.

However, as the council progressed, the pope desired the passage of a doctrine regarding the infallibility of the church, and it came to stand as an essential requirement of the council. Not surprisingly, many Roman Catholic leaders were feeling bruised psychologically, and betrayed by the dis-establishment of the formerly Catholic countries that had been created throughout Europe. They saw passage of the infallibility doctrine as filling a political need as much as a religious one. It could serve as a loyalty oath to bolster a frightened and beleaguered institution.

Since the earliest days of the church, there had been the concept of *indefectibility*, which is the belief that the Holy Spirit would always guide and preserve the church in an ultimate way, by finding the equilibrium that is needed in a world of human frailty. The Holy Spirit would never possibly let the church die, and in that sense, the church itself was infallible. The successes of the early councils were a demonstration of the existence and value of this providential guidance.

During the discussions, the idea of the infallibility of the church being specifically vested in the person of the pope was generally opposed by the bishops from France, Austria, Germany, and the United States. It was supported by most of the Italians, but it was a hotly argued topic.

Cardinal Guidi, Archbishop of Bologna, met privately with the pope and stated strongly that individuals, even popes, are not infallible. Reportedly, Guidi told the pope that while papal teachings could be infallible, when they served to preserve the life of the church, the particular interpretation of infallibility as being specifically invested in the person of the pope would go against tradition, especially the tradition that any sort of infallibility lay in the wisdom of the church as a whole, and especially as it related to the bishops in council. Pius IX's reported retort was, "I am tradition."*

When it became clear that the doctrine would pass, following the traditional spirit of seeking unanimity in council decisions, the bishops opposed to it left; the final vote came on July 18, 1870, and it passed 533 to 2.** (One of the no votes being from the bishop of Little Rock, Arkansas.) The doctrine *Pastor Aeternus* assigned to the pope, "full and supreme jurisdiction of the church in those matters which concern discipline and direction of the church dispersed in the world."

* Bernard and Margaret Pawley, *Rome and Canterbury Through Four Centuries*, p. 229

**Norman Tanner, *The Councils of the Church*, 2001

[23

The effects were immediate. The French troops who had been defending the pope and the council from the competing Italian forces withdrew. The very next day, July 19, 1870, the Franco-Prussian war broke out. The council didn't officially conclude; the bishops just stopped and fled for their lives, without declaring the meeting over or completed. They left the job of clarifying and interpreting the new infallibility doctrine to the canonists, who generally used their influence to strengthen and centralize the power center of Rome.*

*Bernard Barlow, *A Brother Knocking At The Door*, p. 183

Just two months later, on September 29, 1870, Rome itself fell, and the 1500-year papal rule of Rome, and the claim to any of former papal territory ingloriously ended. Popes continued to meaninglessly claim temporal authority until Pius XI and Mussolini signed the Lateran Agreements in 1928, which finally established the independent but tiny Vatican State.

The new doctrine of infallibility dismayed Lord Acton, the famous British historian and Catholic layman, in Rome for the Vatican Council. He wrote to his friend William Gladstone, Prime Minister of Great Britain, that the doctrine "gave him (the pope) an arbitrary power of the most unlimited kind in everything with which he chooses to deal."**

**Letter from March 11, 1870, in Bernard and Margaret Pawley, *Rome and Canterbury Through Four Centuries*, p. 227

This note to Gladstone foreshadowed Acton's most famous line, also in reference to papal infallibility. In a letter to Bishop Mandell Creighton, on April 5, 1887, Acton wrote, "Power tends to corrupt. Absolute power corrupts absolutely."

Lewis Carroll commented on the doctrine of infallibility when the Red Queen, in *Through the Looking Glass*, argues against Alice's appeal to common sense.

"I can't believe that, " said Alice.
"Can't you?' the Queen said in a pitying tone. "Try again: draw a long breath and shut your eyes."
Alice laughed. "There's no use trying," she said. "One can't believe impossible things."
"I dare say you haven't had much practice," said the Queen. "Why, sometimes I've believed as many as six impossible things before breakfast.

Alban McCoy, *An Intelligent Person's Guide to Catholicism*, p. 3

While it has an ultra-rationalistic and dictatorial ring, perhaps especially so to us today, the infallibility doctrine was closely defined. It was to be used only in the realm of faith and morals, and never to be used to break new ground, but rather only to express the already existing mind of the church.

ANGLICANS BECOME A WORLDWIDE COMMUNION

Anglicans were figuring out modernity in their own way, and a segment of the Anglican Church in England, called the Oxford Movement, was looking for renewal in this early modern period of the mid-1800's. They saw the potential for this in the sacramental life of Roman Catholicism.

The Oxford Movement was not a purposeful ecumenical attempt. Rather, its goal was to ignite the spiritual life by returning the Anglican Church to a closer practice of the liturgy and habits of the first years of the early church.

Through their *Tracts for the Times*, begun in 1833, the Oxford Movement, inspired the reintroduction of the Eucharist to Sunday worship, which had come to be centered on Morning Prayer. It also revived religious communities of monks and nuns. A by-product was that it created a clearer understanding of Roman Catholicism for Anglicans, and therefore, a greater familiarity with Roman Catholic life and practices.

One of the primary leaders of the Oxford Movement, the Anglican clergyman John Henry Newman, explored and wrote about the overlapping historical and doctrinal connections between Anglicans and Roman Catholics, and even tried to show in his Tract 90, which appeared in 1841, that the beliefs of Rome and Canterbury were capable of being overlaid without there being many differences. The institutional reception to this was totally negative, which contributed to Newman's eventual departure from the Anglican Church to the Roman Catholic Church.

England had only recently passed the Catholic Emancipation Act (1829), which after almost 300 years finally allowed Roman Catholics to worship freely, and it wasn't until 1850 that the re-establishment of a

Roman Catholic priestly hierarchy was allowed in England. Though many of England's oldest and most prominent families had remained Catholic since the time of Henry VIII, there was a faint impression of disloyalty to England if one was a Roman Catholic. By the same token, the Holy Office in Rome also saw fit to deliver a decree to Roman Catholics in England that ended with the admonishment that Catholics should "not be carried away by a delusive yearning for newfangled Christian unity."*

*E. C. Messenger, *Rome and Reunion,* p. 95

There continued to be a potent evangelical side to Anglicanism, especially in England. It was characterized by a strong witnessing to the social gospel and a de-emphasizing of the ceremonial. It gave hope and a church home to the new industrial workers of the 19th century, and provided general renewal to the church. Vestments, incense, making the sign of the cross, and anything that smacked of high church (read Roman Catholic) symbolized a church that was out of touch with common people and their needs, which was where the church's heart had to be centered.

Odd as this sounds to us today, the result of this intense rubbing of differing emphases in England was the actual imprisonment of at least four clergymen for celebrating mass in too ceremonial a manner, a violation of the Public Worship Regulation Acts of 1874, passed to put down the ritualists. Three men were sent to jail for several months and one, the Rev. Arthur Tooth, for one and a half years.

In concert with the English government's expansion of empire, the Anglican Church was moving out beyond England, and forming missions and churches in newly established countries, from Asia to Africa. Missionaries were sent to these international destinations, and England's homegrown religion was transformed into the worldwide Anglican Communion. These countries were far from home and this was no longer a church on one small island; other cultures and habits had to be reckoned with. New and differing systems of local governance were developed.

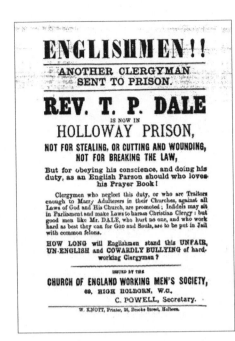

Imprisoned under the Public Worship Regulation Acts of 1874, for having too much ritual.

Princeton Theological Seminary Library

The first worldwide meeting of the newly formed association of the Anglican Communion was held in London, at Lambeth Palace in 1867, two years before Vatican I. One hundred and forty-four bishops attended and it inaugurated these every ten-year convocations for bishops who came from around the world.

Not unlike Vatican I, this first Lambeth Conference was attempting to address questions of authority and governance. The precipitating need for an international meeting had come about after the unilateral action of Bishop John William Colenso of Natal in South Africa. Some of his liberal theological teachings caused a controversy that shook the Anglican Church in Natal, and raised constitutional as well as doctrinal issues all the way to Canterbury. Resolution Four, passed at Lambeth in 1867, said that unity in faith and discipline was best maintained by branches subordinate to higher synods, but there was disagreement about exactly what authority should be given over to the Lambeth Conference.

ECUMENICAL STIRRINGS

After over three hundred years of denominational splintering and alongside the newly secular governments, begun in the United States in the late 18th century and extended throughout Europe in the 19th, and perhaps *because* of this disestablishment, the end of the 19th century exhibited the first stirrings toward some type of re-connection among certain Christian denominations. Within the new secular and pluralistic world, religious communities, particularly the large international institutional religions felt a greater need for each other, especially among the missionaries, and a renewed shared bond.

There had been early lonely calls for ecumenical thinking from some, including William Wake, Archbishop of Canterbury from 1716-1737. He had a ten-year, confidential, (even writing out his own letters) exploratory correspondence with several French Catholic theologians, principally Louis Ellies duPin. Any measurable ecumenical progress at that time was really non-existent - this was one man secretly corresponding with a few French scholars but Archbishop Wake's approach presaged several important principles of ecumenical dialogue.

He saw the divided Christian family as a great human failure, and sought union with Rome, as well as with the Protestants. He didn't think that unity could be based on exact agreement on doctrine or liturgy or discipline, but believed that there could be variable connections from country to country, related to order and discipline, and that there could exist adequate respect and understanding to share communion and to be called one church.

> To frame a common confession of faith, or liturgie (sic), or discipline, for both churches is never to be accomplished. But to settle each so that the other shall declare it to be a sound part of the Catholic Church, and communicate with one another as such; this may easily be done without much difficulty by them abroad, and I make no doubt but the best and wisest part of our Church would be ready to give all due encouragement to it.
>
> G. K. A. Bell, *Randall Davidson,* letter from Archbishop Wake to W. Beauvoir, p. 1255

Archbishop Wake's was an isolated call for closer relations. Over the centuries there had been other friendships, some meetings and a few exploratory letters calling for closer ties, but ecumenism didn't really exist, and the concept or desirability of reunion was too remote for most people to contemplate.

The Lambeth Conference of 1888 was one of the first religious meetings to directly address ideas of Christian unity, and it defined the Anglican approach to it. Based on the writings of the American bishops who had met in Chicago in 1886, it stated the following four basic beliefs to be essential requirements of any discussion about Christian reunion.

· The Old and New Testaments contain all things necessary to salvation.

· The Apostles' Creed and the Nicene Creed are the standard of Christian faith.

· Belief in Baptism and the Eucharist.

· A locally adapted historic episcopate.

In 1889 began the first direct and sustained ecumenical meetings between Rome and Canterbury which were a long series of conversations and writings between Abbe Fernand Portal of Cahors and Paris, and Lord Halifax, an Anglican layman who had been influenced by the Oxford Movement while an Oxford undergraduate. Initially, these were just two men, one Roman Catholic and one Anglican, who met by accident, in Madeira, and through friendly conversation had come to believe that mostly what separated their two churches was a lack of understanding and information.

But since he had his personal doubts about whether Anglican orders were valid, Abbe Portal decided that that area needed to be probed in an official way. In order for Anglican ordinations to be valid, they had to be part of an unbroken line of priestly succession that went back to St. Peter. Rome needed to ascertain that ordinations in the English Church continued this unbroken line of priestly succession.

A papal commission was set up in March of 1896 to deliberate the validity of Anglican ordinations. The resulting apostolic letter, *Apostolicae*

Curae, was released in September of the same year. Anglican ordinations were declared to be 'absolutely null and utterly void.' To the dismay of Portal and Halifax, it was explained that this was due to defects in the 16th century Anglican Ordination rites, and, also, to the *intentions* of those doing the ordaining. The papal bull stated that the 1552 ordinal of Thomas Cranmer "omitted references to the Eucharist as sacrifice and the relationship between sacrifice and the priesthood,"* and that the Anglicans who ordained Matthew Parker as the first Anglican Archbishop of Canterbury in 1559, did not truly consider ordination a sacrament.

*George
Weigel,
*Witness to
Hope,* p. 519

The Anglican response, from the archbishops of Canterbury and York, in 1897 said,

> We firmly believe that we have been truly ordained by the chief shepherd to bear a part of his tremendous office of the Catholic Church, and that the Church of England teaches the doctrine of the Eucharistic sacrifice in terms at least as specific as those of the canon of the Roman Mass.
>
> Responsio *Archipiscoporum Angliae ad litteras apostolicas Leonis Papae XIII, De ordinationibus Anglicanis* (with English translation) London 1897, p. 7

Portal and Halifax exchanged affectionate letters that expressed their disappointment. Halifax wrote to Portal on September 21, 1896 "We tried to do something which, I believe, God inspired. We have failed, for the moment. Your letter is more precious to me that I can possibly say. Troubles shared are already half assuaged."

While they felt their failure, the discussion that they initiated, fostered and nourished, which for most people had seemed either undesirable or impossible, had begun, and at a serious and high level.

A conversation, and perhaps even more importantly, a friendship, had been launched.

CHAPTER FOUR

THE ECUMENICAL ERA GETS UP AND RUNNING (1910–1970)

> Ecumenical theology implies total humility and intellectual honesty; it implies being prepared to be guided into all truth by the spirit of truth. This stance is a permanent crucifixion for the intellect. All philosophical categories are to be used critically, with constant awareness that none can comprehend or circumscribe the fullness of the mystery of Christ. Ecumenical theology implies readiness to be guided into recognizing the presence of the truth, i.e. Christ himself, in forms of expression which may be unfamiliar or even 'alien' at first sight.
>
> (*Dictionary of the Ecumenical Movement, Theology: Ecumenical*, p. 1110)

This passage establishes the gold standard for an approach to ecumenical conversation, and, given human nature and the previous centuries, sets an awfully high bar. Conditions of mutual distrust and star-crossed history would take plenty of talk and time to be worked through, and for the principles of the ecumenical movement to take hold. Minds had to be opened and hearts to be softened before much progress could be made.

But the desire for cross-Christian conversation was heating up, fueled by new scholarship and the rippling effects of modernity. The principle question was what place would the Church occupy in modern life? Would it remain a fundamental necessity informing all parts of life, private and public, or was it going to become merely a cultural add-on?

An emerging awareness of the churches' need for each other and of their shared goals was being felt, and an impetus for exploratory conversation was in the air. The untethering of church and state had contributed to this interest within the different Christian churches for understanding better how they all related to each other. For most, the focus was on how to just get along better, and on how to have a voice in society, more than on any ideas of reunion. But since religion was likely to no longer be one of life's givens, perhaps the warring Christians would be wise to try to relate to each other more respectfully, and possibly to even consider joining forces, not just because this was the right thing to do, but because it would make their work of serving those in need more effective.

1910 saw the World Missionary Conference in Edinburgh, Scotland, which was the beginning. It brought together 1200 delegates, principally English speaking missionaries and the people they worked with, from around the world. Many Americans attended, including the lawyer William Jennings Bryan, and Seth Low, former mayor of New York and President of Columbia University. Led by another American, Episcopal bishop and missionary Charles Henry Brent, they saw the need for comparative study across the religions and while World War I delayed the proposed future meetings, the impetus grew. Large international meetings of Christians were held in Stockholm, Sweden in 1925 and the *Faith and Order Commission* got under way in Lausanne, Switzerland in 1927.

There was a yearning for positive human connections after the despair of World War One. New meetings were organized around *Life and Work* for those interested in working together to address people's practical needs, especially the needs of people in distress. The *Faith and Order* meetings were on a different track, working on doctrinal unity.

Though the Roman Catholic Church was not involved, this was the ushering in of a totally new era in relations among the Christian bodies. It was the ecclesiastical equivalent of the international call for a *League of Nations*. The Orthodox churches were not members either but the Metropolitan Dorotheos of Brussa, the *locum tenes* of the ecumenical see, in 1920, called for more cooperation among Christian institutions in his appeal to create a *League of the Churches of Christ.*

Early in the century, Anglicans were exploring ecumenical conversations in multiple directions and were energetic in all of them. Randall Davidson, Archbishop of Canterbury from 1903 to 1928, personally explored closer connections with the Eastern Orthodox Churches, a freshly discovered place with which Anglicans might have an affinity. Anglicans, at the Lambeth Conference of 1920, issued the *Appeal To All Christian People*, a developed and persuasive document that included the following statements.

> The times call us to a new outlook and new measures. The Faith cannot be adequately apprehended and the battle of the Kingdom cannot be worthily fought while the body is divided, and is thus unable to grow up into the fullness of the life of Christ. The time has come, we believe, for all the separated groups of Christians to agree in forgetting the things which are behind and reaching out towards the goal of a reunited Catholic Church.
>
> The spiritual leadership of the Catholic Church in days to come, for which the world is manifestly waiting, depends upon the readiness with which each group is prepared to make sacrifices for the sake of a common fellowship, a common ministry, and a common service for the world.
>
> We place this idea first and foremost before ourselves and our own people. We call upon them to make the effort to meet the demand of a new age with a new outlook. To all other Christian people whom our words may reach we make the same appeal. We do not ask that any one Communion should consent to be absorbed in another. We do ask that all should unite in a new and great endeavour to recover and to manifest to the world the unity of the Body of Christ for which he prayed.

Randall Davidson sent the document to the Roman Catholic cardinal of Belgium, Cardinal Desiré Joseph Mercier, and the ideas pierced his imagination. Known and respected internationally for the strength he had given his people during the war, and at the request of Abbé Portal and Lord Halifax, who were still determined allies, even after their sharp rebuff regarding Anglican Orders, Cardinal Mercier agreed to host a meeting that would bring together Roman Catholics and Anglicans. It was to be purely a fact-finding endeavor, and their agenda was to be determined as they met and talked.

THE MALINES CONVERSATIONS

Four meetings were held, which ran over several years and were held in Malines, Belgium. The first began on December 5, 1921. They were quietly endorsed at the highest levels of both communions, both orally and in writing by Pope Pius XI. They were thus the first exploratory meetings that addressed unity between the Roman Catholic Church and the Anglican Churches.

It was controversial though about how public to be about the dialogue because at the time of the Malines Conversations, many powerful leaders in both churches viewed the attempt as shocking and wrong headed. This memo from Cardinal Mercier, to the clergy in Belgium, characterizes the complex reactions that the conference was producing.

> Rome neither approved nor disapproved officially but approved, encouraged, approves and encourages confidentially.
>
> John A. Dick, *The Malines Conversations Revisited,* p. 116

The conversations raised the fears of both English Anglican evangelicals and English Roman Catholics. Both groups worked actively behind the scenes, and in the press, to kibosh the conversations. They feared that changes would be declared without taking into account their strongly held and divergent views. They had not been invited, and were fearful of their separate churches losing the teachings that were representative of each group's identity.

Neither the Anglicans nor the Roman Catholics at the Malines meetings approached their work with very clear ideas about what they should be discussing, or what the exact desired outcomes might be. As I've said, they were not representing the institutional opinions of their churches, and they were not there to negotiate on specifics. It was purely exploratory and actually, some of their thinking was quite out of phase with the current popular views in their churches. Canon Moyes, emphatically *not* a participant, represented a certain type of Anglican thinking when he commented at the end of the Malines Conversations, "Perhaps the best thing that comes of such attempts is the lesson that nothing ever comes of them."*

*John A. Dick, *The Malines Conversations Revisited,* p. 139

The working Roman assumption continued to be that any future connection with Anglicans would mean some type of a 'return to Rome,' and the Anglican thinking was that they were very broadly exploring all possible forms of closer international Christian unity.

Cardinal Mercier delivered the most memorable paper of the talks. Written by a Benedictine named Dom Lambert Beauduin, and titled *"L'Eglise Anglicane Unie Non Absorbee, (The Anglican Church, United Not Absorbed)"* it set out to describe a future church in which the Anglican Communion would be fully in communion with the Roman Catholic Church, but would have its own particular flavor.

> He spoke about the current position of Uniate Churches in the Catholic Church and suggested that there could be a similar type of arrangement for the Anglican Church - a patriarchate of Canterbury, in communion with Rome, which would have its own liturgy and canon law.
>
> John A. Dick, *The Malines Conversations Revisited*, p. 141

The Uniate Churches, in full communion with Rome, are primarily several smallish churches, mainly in Eastern Europe and the Middle East, who developed their own separate rites and disciplines in the 5th century while acknowledging papal authority. There is also another group of them from the 17th and 18th centuries, formed when several Orthodox Churches divided. These churches provide a way of thinking about Christianity in terms of branches. The Uniates have different liturgical rites and ordain married men, and yet remain in full communion with the Roman Catholic hierarchy. The question was might their history provide a model for an international Christianity, one that was united, and that also incorporated churches with distinct habits and jurisdictions?

In the end, the gift of the Malines Conversations was a living demonstration that proved that direct ecumenical conversation was possible. Through these men, these two churches were getting to know each other at a personal level, and teasing out and attempting to understand the obstacles to unity. While they clearly had different practices, approaches, and histories, there was convergence. Where exactly was it? And, where it didn't exist, might there still be some way to be united in diversity?

The subject on which they went round and round was papal primacy.

> The Anglicans could accept Roman primacy as a simple matter of fact, and as something that had developed in the course of history. Some

might even consider it reasonable to regard it as a providential development in history, but all this was very different from the Roman Catholic claim to a jus divinum (divine law) for the papacy which the Anglicans could not accept as essential to the being of a true church.

H. R. McAdoo, *Rome and The Anglicans*, p. 209

Anglicans were willing to attest to the indefectibility of the church. Indefectibility, as distinct from infallibility (as was previously described) is the belief that the Holy Spirit will never let the faith or the church die. The Holy Spirit would always be at work in the life of the church and would protect it from any long-term error. But for Anglicans, specific claims for the infallibility of the person of the pope, and the 1854 doctrinal assertions about Mary were add-ons. They could imagine the pope as a very positive historical development and as an international center of unity, but not as someone with universal and determinative power over them.

They could not accept the pope's power as an essential and authentic fundamental because they did not believe it could be proved to be a part of scripture. They believed there could be, and probably should be, a primacy of order and dignity within a strongly collegial setting, but in Anglican thinking, papal primacy and infallibility were too closely rooted in and tied to the ancient divine right of kings, and those days were over.

The meetings at Malines were a necessary stage in a long and new process, and eventually provided inspiration for the Roman Catholic ecumenists who worked at Vatican II. Doctrinally, they went nowhere, but at a human level, a window had been opened and good will was breaking through. That the young monks, who had observed Lord Halifax while at prayer as he visited Abbé Portal, were "impressed with the obvious piety of a heretic," reminds us of the hardened divisions that had existed only a few years previously.*

*H. Hemmer, *Fernand Portal, Apostle of Unity*, p. 24

There was still little deep understanding of each other's theology, but Pope Paul VI was correct when, in 1966, he called the Malines meetings "epoch-making." It was a fresh approach to propose that the two churches should develop a real relationship and that it could be based on something that was not solely related to a return to Rome. They could be friendly and get to know each other, as they studied and compared their doctrines.

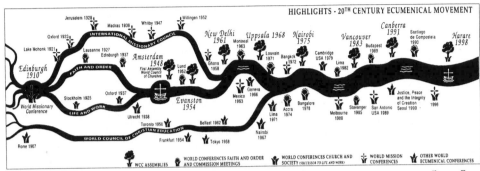

HIGHLIGHTS · 20TH CENTURY ECUMENICAL MOVEMENT

Centro Pro Unione, Rome

WORLDWIDE ECUMENISM AND THE WORLD COUNCIL OF CHURCHES

Ecumenism, as a worldwide movement, was still unknown to most people, and opposed by many in the churches. But more people were beginning to believe that it might be important to think about how to establish better relations among the Christian denominations. This urge began to spawn ecumenical organizations and affiliations from country to country, and denomination to denomination.

The initial leadership for an international ecumenical movement came, perhaps paradoxically, from the Protestants, since a tendency in Protestantism seemed to be to break into new sects when differences arose. The huge Roman Catholic Church had managed to hold together across countries and centuries.

The formation of the World Council of Churches, which was put on hold until the end of the Second World War, joined together the previously mentioned Life and Work and Faith and Order movements. The inaugural meeting in Amsterdam in 1948, and Dr. W. A. visser t'Hooft, was named the first General Secretary.

The World Council of Churches was designed to bring about the reunion of all of the denominations in order to develop the full potential of the impact that an undivided Christianity could have on the world.

In 1956, Dr. Visser t'Hooft wrote,

> Our theologies and particularly our ecclesiologies have not caught up with the new ecumenical situation. There are too few theologians who have woken up to the fact that new answers must be given to the new questions, which have arisen as a result of our ecumenical encounter. And I would like that to be, so far as I have any right to make it, an appeal to the theological faculties of our member churches to take score of the need for much more serious work on this subject.*

*Bernard Leeming, *The Vatican Councils and Christian Unity*, p. 69

There are several examples where local re-union has actually taken place. One is the Church of South India, which was the coming together, in 1947, of Anglican, Presbyterian, Congregational and Methodist churches. Missionaries in India had been galvanized by the 1910 conference in Edinburgh and experienced daily the problems that came with disunity. They agreed to use the Lambeth Quadrilateral as the basis for unity. The main stumbling block was how to maintain the historic episcopate, essential to Anglican orthodoxy. The compromise was to allow the already ordained to be received as ministers and that all new ordinations would be by Episcopal laying on of hands.

Since 1988, the Church of South India bishops, as well as those of North India and Pakistan, have attended Lambeth Conferences as bishops of churches in full communion.

The World Council of Churches has sought unity, but it must be a unity that is based on a large measure of doctrinal agreement on fundamental beliefs. Its work is for the sake of renewal for all, for transforming lives in the world, and it sees sacramental communion as a required goal of reunion. To that end, it has sponsored multi-lateral talks among the major denominations and its most well known accomplishment, from a continuation of the Faith and Order Commission, is the document *Baptism Eucharist and Ministry, the Lima Report,* issued in 1982.

Paragraph 13 of that statement says,

> The words and acts of Christ at the institution of the Eucharist stand at the heart of the celebration: the Eucharist meal is the sacrament of the

body and blood of Christ, the sacrament of his real presence. The church confesses Christ's real, living, and active presence in the Eucharist.

This statement attempts to clarify the meaning of the Eucharist and to clearly place it at the heart of Christian worship and sacrifice.

> That theologians of such widely different traditions should be able to speak so harmoniously about baptism, Eucharist and ministry is unprecedented in the modern ecumenical movement. Particularly note-worthy is the fact that the Commission also includes among its full members theologians of the Roman Catholic and other churches who do not belong to the World Council of Churches itself.*

*World Council of Churches website

BEM is a convergent statement, which sets down what churches can agree about baptism, Eucharist and ministry, and identifies in commentaries the outstanding areas of differences. The amount of agreement recorded is striking.

Today's World Council of Churches, headquartered in Geneva, Switzerland, is the most representative international ecumenical group. Its 348 members are churches representing more than 560 million Christians, from over 110 countries and many cultures, languages and political systems, though the Roman Catholics are still not members. They are however full members of the Faith and Order Commission of the World Council of Churches, and take part in many activities of the WCC. Additionally, there is an active and important joint working group between the WCC and the Catholic Church. The thrust of the World Council of Churches continues to be both service to the world and the reunion of all Christian denominations. The secretary general is the Rev. Samuel Kobia, from the Methodist Church in Kenya.

CHAPTER FIVE

ANGLICANS/EPISCOPALIANS AND ROMAN CATHOLICS INITIATE TALKS AND THE ANGLICAN CENTRE IN ROME OPENS

Though fraught with anxiety on both sides, the quiet and, to many, shocking courtesy visit of Archbishop of Canterbury Geoffrey Fisher to Pope John XXIII at the Vatican in December of 1960, altered the direction of Christian relations in general, and placed Anglican identity squarely in Vatican view. The visit caused consternation: there was fear that it would be given either too much significance or not enough. Curial officials set strict boundaries: there would be no photographs or press releases. In order to broaden the scope of his ecumenical journey and diminish the import of his papal visit, Archbishop Fisher began his trip to Rome by going first to Constantinople, then moving on to Jerusalem, and landing finally in the Eternal City.

This ice-breaking visit was the first of an Archbishop of Canterbury to Rome in over 550 years, since the visit of Archbishop Arundel in 1397, which was 150 years before the formation of the English church. This marked an epic change in the Roman Catholic Church's interest in the Anglican Communion, and its overt interest in all other Christian churches as well, and presaged its ecumenical work at the Vatican II council.

About his meeting, Archbishop Fisher wrote,

> At one point he [the pope] said, 'I should like to read you a passage which included a reference to the time when our separated brethren should return to the Mother Church.' I at once said: 'Your holiness, not return.' He looked puzzled and said, 'Not return? Why not?' I said: 'None of us can go backwards. We are each now running on parallel courses; we are looking until, in God's good time, our two courses approximate and

meet.' He said, after a moment's pause, 'You are right.' This sudden check took him by surprise, but he adapted himself to it at once. This was a notable thing at his age and bore fruit.

William Purcell, *Fisher of Lambeth*, p. 283

Archbishop Fisher was reiterating ideas from the Malines Conversations of forty years earlier when Cardinal Mercier presented the *United Not Absorbed* paper.

The timing of the visit fit in well with a shift that had been underway in Catholic thinking, and which provided the theological underpinnings for these exploratory openings. While several papal encyclicals in the 1940's had maintained the self-contained tendency of official Vatican documents, there was an open tone in the encyclical *Divino Afflante Spiritu*, delivered in 1943.

This notable encyclical recognized that there were different literary genres in the early gospel narratives, thereby opening the door to the possibility of multiple credible interpretations in Biblical research. This created bonds among biblical scholars that crossed denominational lines, as Anglican theologians had also begun to study this and were influenced by the new rational approach to Biblical criticism that had originated in German universities. *Divino Afflante Spiritu* gave credence and significance to the fields of Biblical scholarship and patristic (early church) research.

> This led to a new seeking for the truth of the Biblical stories and to a diminution of the accepted total historicity of the biblical narratives.

Bernard Barlow, *A Brother Knocking At The Door*, p. 180

[41

There were remarkable new discoveries incorporating anthropology, linguistics, philology and history that provided a basis for a renewed appreciation of scripture that would lead to revitalized liturgies and new definitions of what it meant to be a church. Men such as Odo Casel, Henri de Lubac, Louis Bouyer, Jean Danielou and J. A. Jungmann were recognized as providing an historical scriptural basis for adaptations in the liturgies and practices of the churches, which then crossed the denominations.

This maturing of modern Biblical scholarship, which blended academic fields, was entering the Christian blood stream and influencing many churches. Theologians in the Roman Catholic Church were looking freshly at how to use this new information, and at how to interpret it to offer the changeless Christian beliefs in a way that the modern world could hear them.

While Roman Catholics were always members of scholarly societies, in the early 1950's, Roman Catholic Old and New Testament biblical scholars were for the first time allowed to participate in inter-denominational conferences. These were the places where Protestant, Roman Catholic and Anglican leaders and theologians would find themselves on common ground, in their mutual use of this new information, and in their search for renewal that this information would usher in.

The Second World War also influenced the ecumenical scene. Church leaders were intellectually drawn together by calls for unity against a common enemy, and men and women were making connections around the world with people of other Christian denominations and other faiths. Many instances of informal common worship and cross-denominational social programs were taking place, which was a crucial reorientation, and a breaking down of cultural separations. In France, England and the United States, priests, pastors, and laity were actively beginning to work together in labor unions, pacifist and justice organizations, in Mothers' Unions, and for improved race relations.

Pius XII, pope from 1939 to 1958, contributed to the shift in the prevailing state of mind in 1949 with the instruction *De motione oecumenica*. It approved of "congresses of the various denominations to discuss the ways in which we may work in common." Pius XII didn't specifically have reunion on his mind, but it was an opening.

In an individual gesture of friendship, in 1956, Giovanni-Battista Montini, the archbishop of Milan and future Pope Paul VI, hosted ten days of conversation with a group of Anglican clergymen, the purpose of which was mutual familiarization.

While for most Roman Catholics, the vision was still one of return of the Christian world to Rome, world events and Biblical scholarship were opening up Vatican thinking and creating a more fluid situation. These were some of the natural and organic evolutions that led up to the Second Vatican Council, which was called by Pope John XXIII, and which began in 1962.

Vatican II opened up the Roman Catholic Church in an extraordinary way, and raised questions about what was to be the ecclesiology, or nature, of the modern Roman Catholic Church, and what would be its relationship to other Christians and to other faiths. Pondering and wrangling over these questions continues to challenge it today.

The purpose of the Council, as recapitulated by John Paul II, in March of 2000, was "to understand more intimately, in a period of rapid change, the nature of the church and its relation with the world in order to effect an updating."* This did not mean an accommodation to modernity but rather a conversation, an encouraged interaction and involvement with modern lives.

*The Tablet, March 11, 2000

The fallout from Vatican II immediately and profoundly affected the day-to-day life of Catholics around the world because this updating re-centered the heart of the church. Overnight, the laity had a much more central role in the life and identity of the church. They now worshipped not in Latin, but in their own local languages, of which there were hundreds. The sanctuary was opened up and the priest now turned and celebrated the Eucharist while facing the people. This emphasized the freshly imagined identity of the church as being the priest and the people *together*, seeking God's will.

Complex questions were being posed about what was to be the very nature of the church. By placing renewed emphasis on the church *in the world*, and the important transformations that that entailed - developing the concept of the religious rights of all people, reaching out to other Christian churches and other religions, and renewing the emphasis on scripture and liturgy that was based on new research - the Roman Catholic Church was rethinking *how* it was *to be* a church and it was attempting to change itself from within.

To help prepare for the council, Pope John XXIII had, in 1960, established the Secretariat for the Promotion of Christian Unity. He appointed Augustin Cardinal Bea, Jesuit head of the Biblical Institute, to lead it. In his late 70's, Cardinal Bea was most known for his gifts as a spiritual guide, as he had been Pius XII's personal confessor.

It was a surprising choice, but a wise one, because Cardinal Bea was able to be utterly clear that 'no work for union should lead to the neglect of the soundness of one's own faith,' but also that no dogmatic definition could ever fully and totally capture truth. Only by penetrating more deeply into theological principles could human perception of truth grow.

> Truth cannot change but human perception of it can grow in depth and width. The truth revealed by Christ has an undiminished power to teach men lessons which we have not yet learned and accents in which we have not yet spoken.*

*Augustin Bea, *The Unity Of Christians*, Richard Gerald O'Hara in the introduction, p. xiv

This was the first official recognition from Rome that theology was appropriate for comparative study, and events flowed from this re-focusing. The Roman Catholic Church now was extraordinarily attentive to the fact that it was a scandalous situation that the Christian churches were separated, and recognized that they shared some of the responsibility for the partition. The divisions of the 16th century, which in England had been dominated by political considerations, were a mistake on both sides. It was sinful to continue this constant hardening of positions.

The five quite amazing and groundbreaking documents that related to ecumenism, and to the related inter-religious dialogue, to come out of Vatican II were:

Declaration on Religious Freedom (Dignitatis Humanae)
Pastoral Constitution on the Church in the Modern World (Gaudium et Spes)
Dogmatic Constitution on the Church (Lumen Gentium)
Decree on Ecumenism (Unitatis Redintegratio)
Declaration on the Relationship of the Church to Non-Christian Religions
(Nostra Aetate)

The Decree on Ecumenism, the essential ecumenical document of Vatican II, established certain principles. Key was Paragraph 14:

> The heritage handed down by the apostles was received in different forms and ways, so that from the beginnings of the Church it has had a varied development in various places, thanks to a similar variety of natural gifts and conditions of life.

Within the context of addressing Christian communities in the West that grew out of the Reformation, Section 13 in the Decree refers specifically to Anglicans:

> Among those in which some Catholic traditions and institutions continue to exist, the Anglican Communion occupies a special place.

Ecumenically, the most significant development was the new understanding, described in the Decree on Ecumenism (and also in *Lumen Gentium*), that the Roman Catholic Church did not consider itself to be the sole and complete representation of Christianity.

> This church constituted and organized in the world as a society, subsists in the Catholic Church, which is governed by the successor of Peter and by the Bishops in communion with him, although many elements of sanctification and of truth are found outside of its visible structure. These elements, as gifts belonging to the Church of Christ, are forces impelling toward catholic unity.*

Lumen Gentium, 8

On the basis of the *Decree on Ecumenism*, Cardinal Bea, and the *Secretariat For Promoting Christian Unity*, initiated regular dialogue with Christian churches of every stripe.

> At the international level these dialogues were begun with the Anglicans, Lutherans and Methodists soon after Vatican II. With the Presbyterians the dialogue was initiated in 1970, with the Pentecostals in 1972, with the Copts in 1973, with the Disciples of Christ in 1977, with the Orthodox in 1979 and with the Assyrian Church of the East in 1994.
>
> Michael Hurley, *Christian Unity*, p. 32

The Vatican website describes the current state and the historic accomplishments of the multitude of dialogues. The commitment and the resources are significant.

Archbishop Michael Ramsey visited Pope Paul VI in March of 1966, just months after the close of Vatican II. Their *Common Declaration* proposed

> to inaugurate between the Roman Catholic Church and the Anglican Communion a serious dialogue which, founded on the Gospels and on the ancient common traditions, may lead to that unity in truth for which Christ prayed.
>
> from *The Common Declaration*, March 24, 1966

Both Archbishop Ramsey and Pope Paul VI were aware that their creation of an international commission to seek unity would create confounding difficulties and that they were leading their churches into new and unexplored spheres. Their clarity and their confidence was a massive accomplishment and gave purpose, direction and vitality to a dialogue that began in 1967, and that has been progressing ever since.

At the same time, they realized that doctrinal examination wouldn't be enough to bring about reconciliation. A place was needed in Rome where mutual study could begin and familiarity could become second nature. So the Anglican Centre in Rome was founded to give a locus and a heart to this new work of rebuilding relations. Housed in the Palazzo Doria Pamphilj, around the corner from the Pantheon, the Centre offers courses, a research library, a meeting place for ecumenists and pilgrims, worship and hospitality to all comers, but especially to Episcopalians/Anglicans. It celebrated its Fortieth Anniversary in November of 2006. Bishop John Flack is the Centre's current director and the Archbishop of Canterbury's representative to the Holy See.

The *Joint Preparatory Commission* was established, and met three times between January 1967 and January 1968, in Italy, England and Malta. A group of twenty-five Anglican and Roman Catholics made use of the working principles of the Malines Conversations, the ideas of the Vatican II *Decree on Ecumenism*, and were also able to move the discussion forward in fresh ways. Rather than immersing themselves in their differing doctrines and practices, they determined to attempt to define and to reconcile the most basic foundations from which all else flowed, to actually state what they deemed was essential for church unity. They were guided by the principles articulated by Pope John XXIII at the opening of Vatican II. "The subject of the ancient deposit of faith is one thing, and the way it is presented is another."*

*The Final Report, with AAS elaboration, p. 224

The *Joint Preparatory Commission* was able to begin by saying that all Roman Catholics and Anglicans firmly believe that all Christians are specifically united in baptism. Baptismal water links Christians together in a mystical connection to Jesus Christ that cannot be un-done and that exists across the denominations. This was a decisive theological development, and an important one for all of the subsequent dialogues. Seeking a positive platform on which to discuss and explore some version of 'unity by stages,' the 1968 report of the Joint Preparatory Committee was applauded by both churches. The Malta Report emphasized the joint common history that had lasted until 1534, and declared this mutual history to be a firm basis on which to build.

Embedded in the report was a working precept that was a crucial working assumption for a new commission - namely that "divergences since the sixteenth century have arisen not so much from the substance of this inheritance as from our separate ways of receiving it." (Malta Report, Paragraph 4) This was not meant to minimize the differences, but directs any subsequent work toward determining which differences are real and which "merely apparent." (Malta Report, Paragraph 4) They set out a detailed set of suggested actions and stages that were designed to foster closer friendship and agreement.

The Malta Report closed by recommending the formation of a joint international commission that would meet regularly, and that would be directed to find where there was convergence in the faith and life of the two churches, where convergence didn't exist, and, very importantly, to define what was essential to the identity of each church. They had referred to the Vatican Council's references to a "hierarchy of truths"(*Decree on Ecumenism,* 11) and called for the new commission to "examine the questions of authority, its nature, exercise and implications" (Paragraph 22) and they also recommended a study of comparative moral theology. (Paragraph 23)

They issued this striking press release:

> After 400 years of separation between the Roman Catholic and Anglican churches, official representatives from both churches have taken the first steps towards restoring full unity.

William Purdy, The Search for Unity, p. 107

This was the dramatic preparation for the *Anglican/Roman Catholic International Commission (ARCIC)*, which has been meeting annually, since its first gathering at Windsor Castle in January of 1970.

CHAPTER SIX

THE ANGLICAN/ROMAN CATHOLIC INTERNATIONAL COMMISSION BEGINS ITS WORK

There were exceptionally high hopes as this commission began its work, and a genuine belief, on both sides, that they were at the beginning of something entirely new. Each church believed that there was the real possibility that they would be able to perceive in the other a shared faith, which would inaugurate the next stage of a process and that this work would surely be leading to reunion. Given the excitement of the moment and the expectations of and for this group, this was the polar opposite of 'burial by committee.'

Meeting almost every year for the past thirty-five years and against all odds, they've issued nine remarkable agreed documents that lay out the essential building, and stumbling, blocks to union. They've never wavered in their ultimate goal of achieving complete unity between the Anglican and Roman Catholic churches.

The group was asked to closely investigate the language of each other's doctrine, and more importantly, to attempt to understand the intention and the meaning behind it. They were not supposed to make ambiguous or misleading bridges, but they were instructed to avoid the polarizing language that had contributed to the divisions and had thrust their members into opposing camps.

Their conclusions were not expected to be automatically binding on their churches, and while no one knew exactly how their work would be received, it was thought to be the first stage of a new and radical reformulation. It was not easy work, but it was as determined as it was real. Many sections of the documents were "hammered out with sweat and blood."*   *Purdy, *The Search for Unity*, p. 171

> There could be meetings of the Commission where for successive days there seemed to be deadlock with no escape, and in the morning coffee-

breaks walking in the garden one could suddenly be confronted by an archbishop in uncontrollable floods of tears, frustrated by the feeling that the commission was in a gridlock, unable to move forwards, backwards, or sideways.*

*William Purdy, *The Search for Unity*, in Henry Chadwick's Apprecia- tion of William Purdy, p. viii

Sometimes differences of opinion were stronger between members of the same church than along denominational lines. (Clark and Davey, p. 18) There were jokes that only the youngest members would live to see the finished work.

Members of the commission, all men at this point, were chosen for their specific theological, ecumenical and pastoral expertise. Archbishop Ramsey impoliticly declared that, "no ecclesiastical hacks were needed

**Purdy, p. 126

or allowed."** They were named, as well, to represent the differing forces within each church.

> Julian Charley, interviewed at Lambeth, was told that his Grace is eager to have someone who would be able to 'represent in a very definite way the conservative evangelical wing of the Church of England.' He never failed this charge, but things happened to him as to all of us, as they should in dialogue, things that sometimes seemed to terrify.
>
> William Purdy, p. 125

The committee worked with expert advice from historians, canonists, and moral theologians and with support staff, through subcommittee meetings and prepared papers, and through prayer, contemplation, and friendship. Miraculously, the progress they've made is extensive and their agreed statements demonstrate substantial agreement, or close convergence, on the most fundamental beliefs, teachings and practices of both churches.

The Anglican/Roman Catholic Commission has had two stages, ARCIC I and ARCIC II. There were nine Anglican and nine Roman Catholic members of ARCIC I (1970-1981). ARCIC II initially enlarged the group by including women and making it more diverse geographically. In 1991, ARCIC II reconstituted itself as a smaller group with almost all new members.

Meeting at least once a year, for about a week, in such historic and evocative places as Windsor, Canterbury, and Venice, the Roman Catholic and Anglican members of ARCIC I issued four striking documents between 1971 and 1979 and their Final Report in 1981. These statements demonstrated that both churches shared substantial agreement regarding the Eucharist and Ministry and Ordination, and much convergence regarding the meaning and practice of Authority in the churches.

ARCIC I (1970–1981) AGREED STATEMENTS

1971 Windsor, England Agreed Statement on The Eucharist

1973 Canterbury, England Agreed Statement on Ministry

1976 Venice, Italy Agreed Statement on Authority in the Church

1979 Salisbury, England Elucidations of Eucharist and Ministry

1981 Windsor, England Final Report of ARCIC I (Includes Authority II)

In May of 1982, John Paul II made an historic and hugely successful trip to England, the first ever of a Pope, and he and Robert Runcie, Archbishop of Canterbury, initiated ARCIC II. This group has also met annually, and has produced five agreed documents.

ARCIC II (1982–PRESENT AGREED STATEMENTS)

1986 Llandaff, Wales Agreed Statement of Salvation and the Church

1990 Dublin, Ireland Agreed Statement: The Church As Communion

1993 Venice, Italy Agreed Statement: Life In Christ, Morals, Communion, and the Church

1999 Palazzola, Italy Agreed Statement: The Gift of Authority

2004 Seattle, USA Agreed Statement: Mary: Grace and Hope in Christ

Each of these agreed statements is densely packed and closely argued, and was carefully wrought, with an important working precept being the avoidance of polarizing language. The churches have not officially ratified these statements, but neither have they been rejected. Importantly, the Lambeth Conference of 1988 officially received ARCIC I's work, and a Vatican response in 1994 to 'Clarifications' from ARCIC seemed to affirm the content of the statements on Eucharist and Ministry. There have been official responses to ARCIC I's documents, but not so to ARCIC II's, though much of ARCIC II's work was scrutinized before being issued.

As John Paul II confirmed in 1980 at Castelgandolfo,

> You have gone behind the habits of thought and expression born and nourished in enmity and controversy to scrutinize together the great common treasure, to clothe it in a language at once traditional and expressive of the insights of an age which no longer glories in strife but seeks to come together in listening to the quiet voice of the Spirit.
>
> William Purdy, p. 213

Because authority is the most confusing and explosive of the unity issues, I've chosen it to include in the body of this book. The other agreed documents are described in the appendices. As time has passed, the internal workings and changes in both churches have complicated the situation, but the documents, especially those on Eucharist and Ministry, have taken on the presumption of adequately expressing thinking that's been accepted by both churches.

*A. Deneaux, *From Malines to ARCIC,* speech of the then Archbishop of Canterbury George Carey, p. 177

ARCIC's work exists as a jewel, hidden in a vault, waiting to come into the light. It's past time for it to become part of "the lingua franca of the church instead of being the preserve of theologians and professional ecumenists."*

There will always be new issues and internal dissension in each church, but doctrine is not immutable. Unity is so fundamental to Christianity that no problem can be so formidable as to preclude a dialogue that works toward reconciliation.

INTRODUCTION TO AUTHORITY: EARLY LEADERSHIP, PRIMACY, INFALLIBILITY, AND THE CURRENT SITUATION

EARLY LEADERSHIP

During the earliest days of the institutional church, there was obviously no pope. Authority lay with the church councils and the bishops. The early councils were large meetings of leaders, who traveled from their local churches to various regional centers - to Nicea, Constantinople, Arles, etc. The purpose of coming together was to grapple together with the opinions and problems they brought from their respective areas, and then to study the complex whole and to think beyond their local concerns. These representatives were called together to lead the whole group, to provide the over-sight, the epi-scope.

Bringing together the disparate local voices to work together toward agreement for the whole group was crucial to the survival of the primitive church, and it necessitated creative solutions in order to create group cohesion. These councils were an early and important example of the interplay between the local and the universal aspects of the whole, parts that need to be fully entwined and together make up the church.

Gregory of Nyssa had this to report on the popular debate about the Trinity that went on in Constantinople, shortly after the council there in 381.

> If in this city you ask anyone for change, he will discuss with you whether the Son is begotten or unbegotten; if you ask about the quality of bread, you will receive the answer that the Father is greater, the Son is less; if you suggest you require a bath, you will be told that there was nothing before the Son was created!
>
> Norman Tanner, *The Councils of the Church*, p. 46

Early on, certain regional centers came to be more dominant, either because of population or commerce or some type of apostolic history. Five places became the major sees – Rome, Constantinople, Alexandria, Antioch, and Jerusalem.

The patriarchate of Rome began to develop a type of preeminence, though it wasn't intentionally designated as such, and its jurisdiction developed gradually. It seems fair to say that it is really an accident of history that Rome became the central see, and that the bishop of Rome became a type of chief patriarch.

Alexandria, a city that is remote to us today, was huge then and was where the church was most vibrant in its early life. The fundamental teachings of the Trinity and the creeds were conceived and developed there.

But Rome's connections to the apostles were absolute, as it is where Saints Peter and Paul were martyred. It also had, from the earliest days, a good reputation for being insightful about apostolic teachings, and for being fiercely loyal to the teachings of the early councils.

> The first five centuries show us a changeable East, wild for the theological discussions, over against the more sober West.
>
> John Chapman, *Studies on the Early Papacy*, p. 26

Also, the population of the Greco-Roman world was shifting during the 5th and 6th centuries, from East to West, and Rome was becoming not just itself a population center, but the geographical center of things.

POPULATION ESTIMATES / FIRST CENTURY A.D.

Alexandria	400000	Smyrna	75000
Ephesus	200,000 - 250,000	Damascus	45000
Antioch	150,000 - 250,000	London	40000
Pergamum	120000	Athens	30000
Sardis	100000	Jerusalem	20,000 - 50,000
Corinth	100,000 - 200,000	Rome	400,000

Rodney Stark, *The Rise of Christianity* (San Francisco: HarperCollins Publishers, 1997) 131-132. The larger figures for Ephesus, Antioch, and Corinth, as well as Jerusalem, are from Thomas C. Brisco, *Holman Bible Atlas* (Nashville: Boardman and Holman Publishers, 1998) 255, 244, 253, and 228 respectively.

PRIMACY

Scholars debate whether or not some primitive Christians saw Peter as having a supreme type of authority, and whether there are any indications from certain sections of scripture, called the Petrine texts, that he saw himself that way. The local churches and their regional leaders made most of the decisions; only the toughest irreconcilable disputes went to Rome. So the greater power that the bishop of Rome exercised in the early church was that of an arbiter of last resort, which had the effect of his being a unifier at times of serious doctrinal crisis, though it is agreed that this role diminished as time passed.

The concept and practice of the bishop of Rome being the head of the whole church developed sporadically, responding to the needs of the times, and according to the personalities of the person. But, "no simple linear papal progression can be drawn from scripture and church documents."* *Patrick Granfield, *The Limits of the Papacy*, p. 13

And there is

> no direct Biblical proof for the institution of the papacy as a continuing office in the church.
>
> Avery Dulles, SJ, *Resilient Church*, p. 117

Between East and West, there were constant tensions around Roman claims of supreme authority. Orthodox Christians saw the pope as the first Protestant, as a fellow bishop who broke away from the other bishops and the conciliar approach, who over-stepped and claimed a universal power that wasn't his at all, and never could be. (Timothy Ware, *The Orthodox Church*, p. 2) They thought that the bishop of Rome, had slowly, over time, broken away from the essential heart of the teachings of the true church by claiming an absolute primacy. That primacy could belong to the heart of the *whole* church, which was made manifest in the councils, *not* in a person.

To the Eastern Church, the institutional aspects of the church in the West were over-emphasized and it was overly legalistic. In the East, the church was

> not a corpus or institution, somewhat external to its members. It is an organism whose members are one with Christ who is its essence. With this truth enshrined in their language and with a certain avoidance of Western

legalism, the Greeks were able to keep their thought about the one Body more free from the externalizing and institutionalizing tendency.

A. M. Ramsey, *The Gospel and the Catholic Church*, p. 147

These differences were effectively answered a thousand years ago by the mutual excommunication of 1054, and were fully cemented at the sack of Constantinople in 1204. (Though when Constantinople fell to the Turks, in 1453, the final Eucharist celebrated in St. Sophia was shared by Orthodox and Roman Catholic Christians.)

INFALLIBILITY

The doctrine of infallibility, which as a concept first surfaced in the 13th and 14th centuries,* needs to be studied carefully to grasp its meaning, for it is functionally a technical term, and may not mean what it sounds like.

*Brian Tierney, *Origins of Papal Infallibility 1150-1350*, p. 281

As defined in *Pastor Aeternus*, the 1870 document on infallibility from Vatican I, the pope's infallible power is not to declare new dogma or theories, but rather it is, after taking every means possible to ascertain what the teaching sense of the whole church is, is to declare explicitly and authoritatively the truth that *already* exists for the church.

Here is the passage from the doctrine in the 1870 document:

> . . . for the salvation of the Christian people, with the approval of the sacred council, we teach and define as a divinely revealed dogma that when the Roman pontiff speaks ex cathedra, that is, when in the exercise of his office as shepherd and teacher of all Christians, in virtue of his supreme apostolic authority, he defines a doctrine concerning faith or morals to be held by the whole church, he possesses, by the divine assistance promised to him in blessed Peter, that infallibility which the divine Redeemer willed his church to enjoy in defining doctrine concerning faith or morals. Therefore, such definitions of the Roman pontiff are of themselves, and not by the consent of the church, irreformable.

Norman Tanner, *The Councils of the Church*, p. 91

Furthermore, to add clarity, Norman Tanner says,

> the text does not say directly that the pope is infallible. It says, rather, that when the above-mentioned conditions have been fulfilled, the pope 'possesses . . . the infallibility which the divine Redeemer willed his church to enjoy.' In other words, the pope's infallibility is placed squarely and only within the context of the church.

Norman Tanner, *The Councils of the Church*, p. 92

The person in the papal office having this role, or authority, has it solely in order to be the unifier and preserver of the church. He grasps the particular and the whole, and determines an honest and enduring path for the whole church. It is the proclamation that is infallible, not the pope himself, and ultimately any decision, even an infallible one, rests with the acceptance of the whole church.

But the infallibility doctrine has produced unintended confusions. What about known errors of previous periods? What is the status of non-infallible teachings on faith and morals? How is their importance to be gauged? And finally, it is not completely clear which papal pronouncements should be considered infallible.

> It is clear, however, that the church has never issued a list of infallible teachings.
>
> Norman Tanner, *The Councils of the Church*, p. 93

Additionally, from the revised Code of Canon Law in 1983:

> No doctrine is understood to be infallibly defined unless this is manifestly demonstrated.
>
> 1983 Code of Canon Law (RCC) Canon 749, in Norman Tanner, *The Councils of the Church*, p. 93

Anglicans have believed

> that a true and proper understanding of truth and teaching authority in the church is unlikely to be found centered upon one particular bishop, whose judgment can at times be colored by his background and national culture and who, because of this concentration of authority in one person, can escape the checks and balances provided by other norms of authority.
>
> H. R. McAdoo, *Rome and The Anglicans*, p. 267

> The Anglican tradition agreed with Rome that the Church could not err fundamentally, but thought of indefectibility rather than infallibility, and of a multiple authority.
>
> H. R. McAdoo, *Rome and The Anglicans*, p. 250

Indefectibility, as I've explained previously, is the doctrine or belief that God will, over time, preserve the church from error. There may be mistakes and stumbles, but the church's survival is guaranteed; its existence, for all time, is sure. It is a gentler description of authority, but Anglicans see it as the clearest and most honest description of the church's 'infallibility,' which John Macquarrie has called "a persistence toward truth."

The Orthodox believe in a concept of infallibility, but it is their conciliar decisions that they see as infallible. Given their ecclesiology, they do not believe it is right to invest the power of infallibility in one person, but they do believe that when working in a council, certain decrees of the council are infallible.

It is interesting, and important, to note here, that in the 130 years that the doctrine of papal infallibility has been in place, virtually all scholars agree that it has been invoked only once. That was in 1950, and related to Mary. The Marian doctrine, the Assumption of the Blessed Virgin Mary, stated that

> from the universal consent of the ordinary universal magisterium of the church a certain and firm argument is drawn by which the bodily assumption of the Blessed Virgin Mary into heaven is verified and therefore to be believed by all the children of the church.

THE CURRENT SITUATION

The entire concept of infallibility is peculiar in modern rational terms, and it looms large in the public consciousness of Roman Catholic identity. To our modern ears, it sounds sacrilegious to say that a person, or a church, is infallible. It seems to imply a self-existence, a vanity, an eternal omniscience that seems to be too God-like. Who or why would someone believe that a person, even an incredibly wise and holy one, could honestly claim to never make a mistake?

Often, making the pill even more bitter, it is perceived as working in tandem with some of the actions of the Roman Catholic Church that suppress dissent, and that appear to impose a type of intellectual lockdown. The institutional churches are suspect enough, but combine the current Roman Catholic Church with what papal infallibility is perceived to mean, and the situation seems almost dangerous to the postmodern educated person.

But these popular perceptions misrepresent the doctrine of infallibility; maybe we should be open to thinking about whether there might be advantages to having a final voice of authority in the religious world. Maybe infallibility is a confusing choice of words. The way the doctrine functions is akin to our Supreme Court. Just as the Supreme Court hates to reverse itself, a church that claims an infallible voice may be a legitimate attempt at providing a voice that represents, at any given time, a useful mix of faith and reason that is at the deepest heart of the manmade institution called church.

And while it doesn't provide an exact analogy, our use of the death penalty in the United States effectively asserts infallibility. It has been imposed over 4500 times since 1930, and the brute finality of the outcome suggests a belief that the legal judgment was infallible.

Could it be that the doctrine of infallibility is a very specific and rarefied metaphysical assertion, and is actually a more flexible word than irreversible?

> In accordance with the hope expressed by Pope Paul VI, our declared purpose is to re-establish together full unity in legitimate diversity.
>
> *Ut Unum Sint*, Paragraph 57

From John Paul II's encyclical, this implies that the doctrine of infallibility is itself open to a reformulation. For, if infallibility can be historically conditioned, it really doesn't mean what it sounds like.

The bishops at Vatican I passed the doctrine of infallibility in a rushed desperation. The church was in danger.

> The council majority saw the Church besieged from all sides in an almost apocalyptic situation. They were traumatized by the Enlightenment, the French Revolution, the absolutism of modern states, by Gallicanism and Episcopalianism, and wanted to make sure that the church would remain capable of action in an extreme situation. This is why they reverted to the modern idea of sovereignty, enabling him to act even if he should be prevented from communication with the church. So their statements on primacy were conceived for extreme and exceptional situations.
>
> Kasper, Walter, *That They All May Be One, The Call to Unity Today*, p. 145

Infallibility should, therefore, be understood in the limited and abstract conceptual framework in which it is set. Ultimately, infallibility teachings, and even the doctrine of infallibility, can only offer fleeting, partial attempts to be helpful in our attempt to understand the mystery of God and of the gospels, for church teachings, even on infallibility, are inevitably subject to the interpretation of each new age.

CHAPTER EIGHT

CHURCH GOVERNANCE TODAY AND ARCIC'S AGREED STATEMENTS ON AUTHORITY

How authority is viewed and has been used in each of these churches has anchored their very identities and discussion of it has been at the core of the Anglican-Roman Catholic dialogue. It really is the issue, above all others, that causes people to wonder how reunion could ever come about. But stumbling block that authority can seem to be, like other issues ARCIC addressed, progress has been made.

ARCIC I and *II* have produced four agreed documents on authority: *Authority I* (1976), *Authority II* (1981), *Elucidations* (1981) and *The Gift of Authority* (1999). Three important principles were assumed when they wrote them:

- · The conviction that Anglicans and Roman Catholics have things to learn from each other regarding authority, indeed things that they *ought* to learn from each other, in order to exercise the authority given to Christ's church more faithfully and effectively
- · These agreed documents attempt to describe an ideal norm
- · A constant state of reform is required for effective authority in the church

With these assumptions as givens, *ARCIC* presents a developed theology that articulates a balance between the universal and the local centers of the church. It respects and finds a commonality in the history that was shared until the 16th century, and recognizes the positive develop ments that have occurred in each church since those divisions.

INTRODUCTION

Before beginning, it seems important to state the obvious. A person's relationship with a church is a voluntary one. A worshipper chooses on a

Sunday morning whether or not to worship, and where to do it. Someone may be born into a particular religion, but it is his or her choice whether to stay or leave, and to what extent to abide by the teachings and the rules of each church. Of course the numbers of people who go to church every Sunday has diminished, but churches are still strong institutions in the culture. There is also a huge amorphous body of believers, who are very glad that churches exist when they need one – in times of personal or national crisis, and for marriages, births and holidays. It is worshippers, though, who actually will have the power in the end to shape the church because they're the ones who choose to show up, who volunteer, who desire, and who give.

In a political sense, like states, churches also create a form and an order. There are canon lawyers and ecclesiastical courts, but they exist for the rare cases. There are no church prisons.

A church claims authority for itself in order to promote and to foster a life of faith, and to help its members to establish a relationship with God and with others. Before all else, a church claims authority because it believes that Christ has given it a task, a responsibility, and an accompanying authority to carry out that task.

A church's authority is fundamentally a moral authority, and its realm and effectiveness is mysterious to understand, for it demonstrates the ultimate paradox of Christianity. The authentic practice of Christianity has to be chosen freely and lived out, but for that life in faith to *mean* anything, there needs to be a certain level of confident submission - of acknowledging that the Church's authority is legitimate and willed by God. Saying yes to baptism and to the creeds will mean a relationship with some pattern of Godly authority, which is located in a churchly organization.

For sure, a church's authority and its system of governance also exist to ensure its survival. But authority only takes hold and sticks when the leaders and the people, with developed and informed consciences, live out the potential that the church presents for developing a deeper connection to God, recognizing that they submit to this authority in perfect freedom. The question now becomes how the institutional churches believe this authority is most truly, authentically and usefully ordered. A productive discussion of authority, in any realm, let alone that of the institutional church, is difficult today, and both churches have been wrestling with the best ways to organize themselves internally.

THE TOP LEADER

It may surprise certain readers to learn that John Paul II was concerned about the difficulties that the papacy holds for many Christians, and in his 1995 encyclical, *Ut Unum Sint (That They All May Be One),* he goes outside of his church to ask for help to

> find a way of exercising the primacy which, while in no way renouncing what is essential to its mission, is nonetheless open to a new situation.
>
> *UUS,* Paragraph 95

He declared that the very nature of the papacy of the future was an *open question for all Christians,* especially theologians and pastors, and asked for assistance in thinking about a reformed papacy.

Cover of John Paul II's 1995 encyclical on ecumenism
Libreria Editrice Vaticana

ENCYCLICAL LETTER
UT UNUM SINT
OF THE HOLY FATHER
JOHN PAUL II
ON COMMITMENT
TO ECUMENISM

This is an immense task, which we cannot refuse and which I cannot carry out by myself. Could not the real but imperfect communion existing between us persuade Church leaders and their theologians to engage with me in a patient and fraternal dialogue on this subject, a dialogue in which, leaving useless controversies behind, we could listen to one another, keeping before us the will of Christ for his Church and allowing ourselves to be deeply moved by his plea 'that they may all be one . . . so that the world may believe that you have sent me? (John 17:21)

UUS, Paragraph 96

In earlier days, popes were not merely spiritual leaders but also powerful secular rulers, marrying off their nephews, nieces, and illegitimate children, in order to form controlling alliances, and to further their temporal control. Sometimes, they've been gifted spiritual and theological unifiers and leaders who spearheaded pivotal moments in the church, and protected people against state oppression.

The papacy is esteemed for its role in civilizing the barbarian nations and it is condemned for establishing the barbaric Inquisition. Portrayed as the conscience of Europe, its own political activity has often been Machiavellian.*

*Patrick Granfield, *The Papacy in Transition,* p. 1

There is no job description for the pope. He is not a manager or a monarch. He has the extraordinarily byzantine job of unifying the disparate cultural interpretations of the teachings of this mega, worldwide church and of deciding the hard cases. At root, his power, and that underlying the church, since it is a voluntary association, is the power to inspire hope and belief, to maintain unity in faith and uphold appropriate diversity. He gives a face and a reality to a system that is built on a mystery, something that can never be fully defined or grasped.

All large, institutional churches have some type of decision-making authority, some person or group where the hard, final decisions are made. This is where the responsibilities are to the whole body of the faithful, so a form of primacy exists when a church is large and particularly when it is international. The bonds may be loose though, as they are say for Lutherans or the Reformed Churches.

So, as a *principle*, primacy is used and accepted in the Roman Catholic, the Orthodox, and the Anglican churches, while it means something different in each. These churches have similar systems of priests, bishops and regional leaders, but only the Roman Catholics have a strong international unifying head in the person of the pope (Benedict XVI is the 265th pope), who works in concert with the College of Bishops. They are aided by the Roman Curia, the administrative offices in Rome which are responsible for maintaining different aspects of the Church's unity and mission, and which consists of fewer than 3000 people. "The Catholic Church is about the most decentralized institution in the world," said the Rev. Thomas Williams, dean of theology at Regina Apostolarum Pontifical University in Rome. " There are 1.1 billion Catholics and 2,600 employees at the Vatican. The proportion would be like to run the federal government of the United States with 500 people."*

*New York Times, February 25, 2005

CHURCH ORDER

Several boards, under papal direction, administer the Vatican State, the secular government of the Vatican, and they include lay members. The Holy See, which oversees the worldwide church of over one billion people, of the Latin Rite, and the differing Oriental rites, is lead by the pope and the Curia. The pope currently appoints almost all of the bishops, who then fan out to be fairly autonomous administrators, within the bounds of church teaching, as leaders at the regional and local levels. While there is wide room for theological speculation and development in the Roman Catholic Church, the pope is the teaching voice of the church and his writings are given the presumption of truth.

For the last thirty-five years, the Anglican Communion has been clarifying and strengthening its international bonds of union. While the first Lambeth Conference was held in 1867, the Anglican Consultative Council, which brings together bishops, clergy and laity, was only constituted in 1970, and the Primates, at this point there are 38 of them from around the globe, only began to meet biannually in 1986.

Anglicans look to the Archbishop of Canterbury as their chief leader, but his power is historically and most fundamentally in the moral realm, and his authority comes from the respect that he earns by his holiness and by his skills of leadership and persuasion.

The Anglican Church in Aotearoa, New Zealand & Polynesia
The Anglican Church of Australia
The Church of Bangladesh
Igreja Episcopal Anglicana do Brasil
The Episcopal Church of Burundi
The Anglican Church of Canada
The Church of the Province of Central Africa
Iglesia Anglicana de la Region Central de America
Province de L'Eglise Anglicane Du Congo
The Church of England
Hong Kong Sheng Kung Hui
The Church of the Province of the Indian Ocean
The Church of Ireland
The Nippon Sei Ko Kai (The Anglican Communion in Japan)
The Episcopal Church in Jerusalem & The Middle East
The Anglican Church of Kenya
The Anglican Church of Korea
The Church of the Province of Melanesia

La Iglesia Anglicana de Mexico
The Church of the Province of Myanmar (Burma)
The Church of Nigeria (Anglican Communion)
The Church of North India (United)
The Church of Pakistan (United)
The Anglican Church of Papua New Guinea
The Episcopal Church in the Philippines
L'Eglise Episcopal au Rwanda
The Scottish Episcopal Church
Church of the Province of South East Asia
The Church of South India (United)
The Anglican Church of Southern Africa
Iglesia Anglicana del Cono Sur de America
The Episcopal Church of the Sudan
The Anglican Church of Tanzania
The Church of the Province of Uganda
The Episcopal Church in the USA
The Church in Wales
The Church of the Province of West Africa
The Church in the Province of the West Indies

Henry Chadwick describes the situation.

> We have seen that the Lambeth Conference was allowed to be founded only if it has no authority. But meetings start to gather authority if they exist and are seen not to be a cloud of hot air and rhetoric. It was impossible that the leaders of the Anglican Communion should meet every ten years and not start to gather respect; and to gather respect is slowly to gather influence, and influence is on the road to authority. It continued to have that absence of legal authority which some of its founders wanted and which by necessity was denied to them. But in most Churches some of the most important parts of authority are not based on the law.

> *Resolutions of the Twelve Lambeth Conferences,* 1867-1988,
> Introduction by Henry Chadwick, p. x

International meetings of Anglican primates and bishops and internal doctrinal commissions have been and are wrestling with the best ways for the Anglican Communion to be connected. The Lambeth Conference, in 1998 passed Resolutions III.6 and IV.13 which, though non-binding, call for the Archbishop of Canterbury to lead the whole communion and, when needed, to exercise oversight in extraordinary cases. Indeed, the Lambeth Commission of Communion (2004), lead by Robin Eames, Primate of All Ireland, was charged with clarifying or answering when it might be appropriate for the Archbishop of Canterbury to get involved in any of the 39 provinces of the Anglican Communion and suggest specific ways to strengthen the ties.

A REFORMED PAPACY

The papacy is a particular form of episcopal leadership, but since there is no agreement, and has not been for a very long time, about the scope of papal leadership and whether it is historically and biblically integral to the very essence of what it means to be a church, the question is *how* the papacy should be exercised in an ecumenical, and pluralistic, world.

It is relevant to point out that what Benedict XVI said, as Cardinal Josef Ratzinger, and the then President of the *Congregation of the Doctrine of the Faith*, was that the Orthodox Church

> share with us [Roman Catholic] the conviction of the necessity of the apostolic succession; they have a genuine episcopate and Eucharist. But they cling to the idea of autocephaly, according to which the Churches, even if they are united in faith, are also independent from one another. They cannot accept that the Bishop of Rome, the Pope, is the principle and center of unity in a universal Church understood as communion.

> Vittorio Messori, *The Ratzinger Report*, p. 162

ARCIC makes it clear that Anglicans are not a priori opposed to a visible and personal focus of unity at the world level. (*Authority I*, Paragraph 23; *Authority II*, Paragraph 9; *Gift of Authority*, Paragraph 60) They do object to basing the claim for primacy solely on biblical references to Peter, and on any use of language that claims the papacy to be by divine right, meaning existing directly because of and from the power of God. They have objections also to the doctrine of infallibility and to immediate papal jurisdiction. This is covered most thoroughly in *Authority II*, Paragraphs 5, 6, 11, and 12.

ARCIC's agreed statements find a reformed papacy to be the most fitting place for an international center of Christian unity at this time. (*Authority II*, Paragraph 9)

As the future Archbishop of Canterbury Michael Ramsey wrote, back in 1936,

> A papacy which expresses the general mind of the church in doctrine, and which focuses the organic unity of all the bishops and of the whole church, might well claim to be a legitimate development in and through the gospel. But a papacy which claims to be a source of truth over and above the general mind of the church and which wields an authority such as depresses the due working of the other functions of the one body, fails to fulfill the main test.
>
> A. M. Ramsey, *The Gospel and the Catholic Church*, p. 65

The key for Anglicans rests on the nature of a modernized papacy and on how Anglican identity, history and independence would work within a reformed relationship. What exists today has evolved over time. Any rapprochement would require a long, slow process with clear criteria.

> Anglicans are entitled to assurance that acknowledgment of the universal primacy would not involve the suppression of theological, liturgical and other traditions which they value or the imposition of wholly alien traditions.
>
> *Authority II*, Paragraph 22

In Paragraph 54 of their response to *Ut Unum Sint*, the Anglican bishops in England quoted Cardinal Ratzinger, now Benedict XVI, when he spoke on the communion between the Roman Catholic Church and the Orthodox churches.

> As far as the doctrine of primacy is concerned, Rome must not require more of the East than was formulated and living during the first millennium.

The Lambeth Conference, in 1988, welcomed *ARCIC's Final Report*.

> Authority in the Church (I and II) together with the Elucidation, is a firm basis for the direction and agenda of the continuing dialogue on authority and [the Lambeth Conference] wishes to encourage ARCIC II to continue to explore the basis in Scripture and Tradition of the concept of a universal primacy, in conjunction with collegiality, as an instrument of unity, the character of such a primacy in practice, and to draw upon the experience of other Christian churches in exercising primacy, collegiality and conciliarity.
>
> Resolution 8

THE LOCAL AND THE UNIVERSAL

A central topic of all of the *ARCIC* authority documents is the relationship of the local church to the universal church, which is really the central question going forward. Do the local churches, Roman Catholic and Anglican, believe that they are part of a universal, international church, and how will they organize a shared leadership?

> A local church cannot be truly faithful to Christ if it does not desire to foster universal communion, the embodiment of that unity for which Christ prayed.
>
> *Authority I,* Paragraph 13

Many people within the Roman Catholic Church who favor reforming the papacy have centered on making church leadership more collegial, and using the concepts of subsidiarity and a more dispersed leadership to better effect. John R. Quinn, the retired archbishop of San Francisco, responded to John Paul II's request for a dialogue on the papacy in his books *The Reform of the Papacy* and *The Exercise of the Papacy.*
In them, he calls on his lifetime of experience as a leader in the church to respectfully explore some of the many practical ways of creating a more collaborative and consultative papacy,

> one that respects legitimate church structures such as the patriarchates and episcopal conferences, and one that is dedicated to preserving diversity with the framework of unity.
>
> John R. Quinn, *The Reform of the Papacy,* p. 29

Organizational strife in the church is not new to our age. In the early 1400's, the papacy was threatened with schism as three different men in three different cities (Rome, Avignon, and Arles) claimed to be pope. The Council of Constance, held from 1414-1418, resolved this by affirming the role of the general ecumenical councils.

> In its decree Haec sancta, the Council affirmed that it was a general council representing the entire Church with the authority of Christ. It asserted that its authority was superior to that of any of the faithful, including the pope himself... The theory of conciliarism had been widely discussed by canonists and theologians for two centuries before Constance. But at the council it was put to the test and it was triumphant. It ended the schism.
>
> Patrick Granfield, *The Papacy in Transition,* p. 8

Shortly thereafter, however, 'conciliarism' was challenged, and the papacy was again affirmed as carrying an authority, which could not be overturned by councils.

Again, in the 19th century, with the general disestablishment of church and state, the thrust of the leadership of the Roman Catholic Church changed, becoming more centralized and adding the claim of papal infallibility at Vatican I in 1870.

And today, Roman Catholic bishops in Asia, where about 60% of humanity lives, and which is a fast growing part of the Roman Catholic Church, have been particularly challenging to the Roman hierarchy. The collegial process becomes more and more complex as far-flung growth requires indigenous interpretation and local respect, particularly in Asia where Buddhist habits of non-confrontational and individualized solutions have so affected the church's work. And where the political leadership in China asserts its right to home bishops without consulting the Vatican.

Vatican II reconnected the bishops to the bishop of Rome, and reminded the whole church of the roles and responsibilities of the regional and local church. Pope Paul VI, in 1965, initiated bishops meetings in Rome and bishops have continued to come to Rome and to advise John Paul II and now Benedict XVI. In many places, the Roman Catholic Church has been trying to strengthen local structures and national and regional episcopal conferences, though the responsibilities of national councils of bishops is not always clear.

Paragraphs 19-23 in *Authority I* discuss the important role of bishops in the make-up of churchly authority.

> The bishops are collectively responsible for defending and interpreting the apostolic faith. The primacy accorded to a bishop implies that, after consulting his fellow bishops, he may speak in their name and express their mind.
>
> Paragraph 20

> At the same time, primacy "does not seek uniformity where diversity is legitimate, or to centralize administration to the detriment of local churches.
>
> Paragraph 21

If God's will for the unity in love and truth of the whole Christian community is to be fulfilled, this general pattern of the complementary primatial and conciliar aspects of *episcope* serving the *koinonia* of the churches needs to be realized at the universal level. The only see which makes any claim to universal primacy and which has exercised and still exercises such *episcope* is the see of Rome, the city where Peter and Paul died.

> It seems appropriate that in any future union a universal primacy such as has been described should he held by that see.
>
> Paragraph 23

The cover-up of the pedophilia cases in the United States, and the associated issues regarding church structure, have demonstrated a failure of leadership, not across the board, but by more than a few bishops. The complexity and the difficulty of administrating this huge church, across cultures, languages and local histories is profound and while it works surprisingly well, something failed the faithful in the American Catholic institutional system, and in a few other places worldwide. Even though it was fundamentally a failure at the diocesan level, with such a centralized leadership, the pope and the curia must share the responsibility. Fully understanding what went wrong and why it is important for American Catholics and will be especially so if there are any further leadership gaps.

The most recent agreed *ARCIC* document, the *Gift of Authority*, was issued in May of 1999. It further develops the nature and purpose of authority and uses a scriptural image from II Corinthians 1:18-20 to frame the discussion. By his creation of the world, God has said *Yes* to humanity in an abundant and awesome way. The only possible response from the world is an *Amen*.

The *Gift of Authority* then places this confident *Amen* within the human institution of the church, and suggests that it is most fully real and strong when a clear teaching voice is present. " . . . authority rightly exercised is a gift of God to bring reconciliation and peace to humankind."*

Gift of Authority, Paragraph 5

At the end, in Paragraph 60, it suggests that *both* churches need to re-receive the gift of a *reformed* universal papal leadership and that this would be healing. It is a confident document that has brought out differing responses. It is criticized as being not useful to people because it states an ideal and is therefore out of the realm of practical experience of worshipers, and it's accused of being overly willing to accept theology from above without working it out locally.

The essential question that *The Gift of Authority* poses to the Roman Catholic Church today is how the pope and the Curia will be related to the bishops, the local church and to the faithful. It will be interesting to follow this because with fewer priests in the United States, more and more of the laity are taking pastoral and teaching roles. Lay employees in the church actually outnumber priests already. Unlike the ordained, they are trained, and hired and fired locally and do not have direct ties to Rome, so presumably by definition their loyalty will be more tied to the local church.** *Peter Steinfels, *A People Adrift*, p. 331

Rowan Williams, the Archbishop of Canterbury, has said that the authority of a bishop is "an authority to unify." Bishops need to be clear about their own opinions, but in the end, it is the bishop's role to understand the sense of the whole group, and to lead and to maintain unity after any decisions are made. This is effectively the model inherited from the Council of Nicea.

The *Virginia Report*, presented to Anglican/Episcopal leaders at the Lambeth Conference in 1998, asked whether Anglicans can "go on as a world Communion, with morally authoritative, but not juridically binding decision-making structures at the institutional level." It recommended strengthening the instruments of over-sight and decision-making when it would be helpful for holding the Anglican Communion together. The *Gift of Authority* supported this and both reports have provoked controversy and discussion in the communion, and the ideas have not yet been fully debated.

The Church of England's bishops' response to *Ut Unum Sint* noted the following:

> As ARCIC I pointed out, a serious imbalance may occur when either primacy or conciliarity is emphasized at the expense of the other. This danger is increased when churches have been separated from one another. The koinonia of the churches requires that a proper balance be preserved

between the two with the responsible participation of the whole people of God. In the Church of England and other Anglican churches the principle of conciliarity is firmly embedded in constitutional forms whereby bishops, clergy and laity all play a part in the governance of the church at every level. Bishops retain a special authority in questions of doctrine and worship.

House of Bishops, England, p. 11

CONCLUSIONS

What is successful authority in the religious realm, and how can it be measured? By compliance and obedience to church teachings? Holiness? Size of flock? Relationships with others, and especially with the poor? Service? Personal conversion? Spiritual discernment? Unity?

Obviously holiness cannot be measured, but a church's authority is working at a high level when its members' commitment and belief is active and vital, when religious confidence is high and religious maturity deep.

For authority to be real, it has to be rooted in and framed by its purpose and its purpose has to be rooted in communion and in service. There is no model for a contemporary ecumenical primacy, but without a clear source and true purpose, it could never work. *ARCIC* says sharply that both churches need to reform how they govern themselves.

For many 21st century Westerners, Roman Catholic and Anglican, the centralization of the Roman Catholic leadership seems to be out of step, and to be part of an antiquated cultural world. It doesn't fit with the times. However, in the end, in its utter and prophetic practicality, the leadership of the Roman Catholic Church, centered in the papacy, has always listened and changed *eventually*, according to its worldly, concrete needs.

There is internal dissension in the Catholic Church at this moment, and many faithful Roman Catholics take the pope and the Curia with a grain of salt. They may be scorned as 'cafeteria Catholics' by some, but they consider themselves to be faithful Catholics, who feel they have no choice given their life experiences, but to make their moral decisions while moving in and outside of official church teaching.

Roman Catholics tend to stay in their church even when they are 'out of phase' with the authorities. Some leave, and some of those migrate to the Episcopal Church, but most don't. While this can seem hypocritical to Episcopalians, many Roman Catholics can live with questions and doubts about some church teachings and about internal church administration problems because of the deep felt hope heard explicated every Sunday, and being a partner in the long history of unity.

As I have thought about this, it doesn't seem to me that the problem of papal authority for Anglicans is fundamentally about infallibility, because infallibility is so tightly defined and, though it could be used again, it is, for all intents and purposes, never used. For Anglicans though, if infallibility were upheld, time would have to be given for any decision to be received by all of the faithful.

A problem to be wrestled with is the meaning of the immediate teaching jurisdiction of the pope. There needs to be confidence in the right balance, between honest theological inquiry and dissent, and the honor and 'presumption of truth' traditionally given to the pope. Who will determine when conscience-driven dissent become heresy?

There are embedded and life-sustaining differences in each church that could be lived with and shared by the other. If a fresh re-association were to be a good thing, what would it look like? What would authority look like? What are new relationships that are capable of growing into ever-fuller communion? These are some of the questions that should be probed and the laity should be invited into the conversation.

Perhaps, at this moment, in this global, cross-national world, at this time when nations and people can be over-shadowed or over-run by the efficiency of the trading systems, the allure of cultural products, and the reflexivity of the media, a quiet and visible expression of unity centered in someone, somewhere in the world would be a good thing.

If the pope's expressions in *Ut Unum Sint* are genuine and the Roman Catholic hierarchy is serious about seeking help in reforming the papacy, and if there were clear and positive advantages to breaking out of the negative modern and post-modern impressions of the papacy, this might be the right time for exploring some type of a reformed international papal leadership.

Archbishop Robert Runcie described being at Assisi, the ecumenical and inter-faith gathering for peace organized by John Paul II, in 1986, to the bishops at the 1988 Lambeth Conference.

> Whether we like it or not there is only one Church, and one bishop who could have effectively convoked such an ecumenical gathering. At Assisi I saw the vision of a new style of Petrine Ministy – an ARCIC primacy rather that a papal monarchy. Pope John Paul welcomed us – including other Anglican primates ... but then he became in his own words a brother among brothers
>
> Mary Tanner, *Unpacking The Gift*, p. 31

*Patrick Granfield, *The Papacy in Transition*, p. 1

Historian Arnold Toynbee called the papacy "the greatest of all Western institutions."* Throughout its 2000-year history, it has been an object of love, hate, adoration, misunderstanding and fear. But whether one responds or not to John Paul II, Benedict XVI, or to any particular pope, a reformed papacy is an asset that the world could benefit from. Internationally known religious leaders can serve an increasingly important role in our world.

Because, as Rowan Williams had planned to say in New York on September 12, 2001,

> Pastoral authority is the capacity to bring holiness to birth in another.
>
> Rowan Williams, Hobart Lecture, September 12, 2001, not delivered.

WHAT'S NEXT ?

Theological discourse can seem like sorting angels on the head of a pin, but it actually hasn't been a bad place to begin a difficult, forward-looking task, and while their work is not broadly known yet, *ARCIC* has produced material that will break us out of stereotypes. They've created the underpinnings for a new age. Its likely that they themselves weren't sure what was possible when they began, but their documents and the new climate that they and others have pioneered have gotten us over a high hurdle: the belief that doctrinal agreement on many issues actually exists. They've proved that doctrine, knowledge, and identity even, is formed during the mutual probing and exchange of ideas, and through the give and take of argument and discussion, that happens in conversation. Even critics have recognized that the *ARCIC* documents have clarified old misunderstandings and have prepared the way for something new.

Vatican II specifically mandated this work toward unity for Roman Catholics, and the pursuit of it has become second nature for international leaders, where friendly candor and an honest closeness has had a chance to build up. Of course there have been setbacks, but the people in the pew still need to know of this work, this no-going-back approach, this build up of honest exchange, mutual affection, and trust.

> He (Benedict XVI) is more familiar with ecumenical dialogue than most of his predecessors. His countercultural stand may impel him to make common cause with all who call on Christ's name. And he has a treasure trove of significant agreements with many churches that his office approved. If these agreements were now to be officially implemented, ecumenical dialogue would take giant steps in the next years.
>
> Margaret O'Gara, *Commonweal*, July 15, 2005, p.11

NOTHING MORE THAN NECESSARY

From the beginning, *ARCIC's* charge has come from *Acts15:28*:

> For it has seemed good to the Holy Spirit and to us to impose on you no further burden than these essentials.

ARCIC has believed that an ecclesiology exists that can accommodate different approaches and that separate teachings in certain areas can be held without impairing what is most fundamental. Both churches agree that history and local experiences shape what it means to be a church and that local enculturation is necessary to the health of the church. For Anglicans, this may even mean that different experiences, province to province, might allow for differing scriptural interpretations. The question is what should the limits be? Defining these limits is powerfully complex, and Roman Catholics and Anglicans/Episcopalians obviously start from different places.

It is important to note that classical Roman Catholic theology tends toward the Platonic and believes and teaches that human society works best when it flows from an ideal, from the universal to the particular. Its leaders base their teachings on humanity as it is in its most perfect state and on coherence and unity.

> Although this is a difficult point for many Anglo-Saxons to grasp, when the Vatican makes statements like "no gays in the priesthood," it doesn't actually mean "no gays in the priesthood." It means, "As a general rule, this is not a good idea, but we all know there will be exceptions."
>
> John L. Allen, Jr., *The New York Times*, September 27, 2005, Op-Ed page

This doesn't imply that gays and lesbians are second-class citizen – rather that at an "ideal level," their inability to procreate means that their lives are diminished in that ultimate sense.

Classical Anglican teaching, on the other hand, derives from Aristotle and begins with the individual, with the particulars of each person. Only then does it flow out to the group, and the universal. Both churches live in and serve the world, but Rome attaches itself more closely to an ideal, to something not quite of this world.

THE BATON IS PASSED

At the 75th Anniversary of the Malines Conversations, in 1996, momentum built to find some way to recognize the significant progress that has been made and to move the dialogue beyond the theological realm; the institutional church stepped up.

Rome and Canterbury brought together, in Mississauga, Canada, in 2000, thirteen pairs of English speaking bishops. These pairs of Roman Catholic and Anglican bishops spent a week getting to know each other and studying the *ARCIC* documents. They traveled from India and Ireland, the US and Papua New Guinea, Nigeria and Australia, and so on. They grasped the importance of *ARCIC's* work and were converted. Very importantly, they formed a new group to work on how to introduce *ARCIC's* documents to the local church.

This group, called the *International Anglican Roman Catholic Commission on Unity and Mission (IARCCUM)*, has had three sub-committees at work, but primarily they're drafting a statement that will explain the extent of the theological agreement that *ARCIC* has established, and will help the reception of the agreed documents through mutual study and understanding. They were preparing for its release when word of the election, confirmation and subsequent consecration of Gene Robinson, a priest in a long-term homosexual relationship, to be the bishop of New Hampshire, made headlines across the world.

Bishop Robinson's election caused *IARCCUM* to temporarily pause while both churches pondered what this new development would mean, for each separately, and for the ecumenical dialogue. Bishop Robinson's election has brought to the fore earlier issues, including women's ordination and issues concerning human sexuality here in the United States and internationally, that had unsettled some people for years, but no galvanizing event had previously made them so prominent that they could not be ignored.

The *IARCCUM* subcommittees however continued to work, and at the creative request of Rowan Williams and Cardinal Walter Kasper, President of the *Pontifical Council for Promoting Christian Unity*, an ad hoc sub-committee from *IARCCUM* reflected on what *ARCIC's* work might have to offer the Lambeth Commission on Communion, a group that was established to advise the Anglican Communion and the Archbishop of Canterbury at this unstable and fractious moment in the Anglican Communion.

IARCCUM's ad hoc committee's report to the Anglican Communion came out in June of 2005. It states that the work of bishops is "seriously affected if the majority of bishops in the Anglican Communion will neither receive or recognize the ministry of the bishop of New Hampshire." They ask whether "when new questions arise which in fidelity to Scripture and Tradition, require a united response, will these structures assist Anglicans to participate in the sensus fidelium with all Christians?" And most importantly they ask, "Is the Communion open to the acceptance of instruments of oversight which would allow decisions to be reached that, in certain circumstances, would bind the whole Church?"

This report has come on the heels of *ARCIC II's* final agreed document, *"Mary: Grace and Hope in Christ,"* which was released in May of 2005. The assumption has been that there will be an *ARCIC III*, and the expectation is that their work will delve more deeply into ecclesiology and that they will explore the relationship between the local and the universal church.

Just as things were beginning to settle down, and ecumenical work was getting back on track, two developments rocked the scene. The first happened in June of 2006, at the General Convention of the Episcopal Church in Columbus, OH. The US church surprised the world, and itself, by electing a dark horse candidate, Katharine Jefferts Schori, a scientist and the Bishop of Nevada, to be the leader of Episcopalians in the US. This meant that she would be the first woman to lead one of the 38 provinces of the Anglican Communion, not all of whom ordain women. To complicate matters, she had also voted to approve Gene Robinson's election.

Then, in England, not two weeks later, the equivalent body decided that there was no theological reason that women priests in England could not become bishops.

Rowan Williams, Archbishop of Canterbury and leader of the Anglican Communion, has been clear about how precarious the situation is. What follows are excerpts from a long meditation he sent to the Anglican Communion on June 27, 2006.

> There is no way in which the Anglican Communion can remain unchanged by what is happening at the moment. Neither the liberal nor the conservative can simply appeal to a historic identity that doesn't correspond with where we now are. We do have a distinctive historic tradition - a reformed commitment to the absolute priority of the Bible for deciding doctrine, a catholic loyalty to the sacraments and the threefold ministry of bishops, priests and deacons, and a habit of cultural sensitivity and intellectual flexibility that does not seek to close down unexpected questions too quickly. But for this to survive with all its aspects intact, we need closer and more visible formal commitments to each other. And it is not going to look exactly like anything we have known so far. Some may find this unfamiliar future conscientiously unacceptable, and that view deserves respect. But if we are to continue to be any sort of 'Catholic' church, if we believe that we are answerable to something more than our immediate environment and its priorities and are held in unity by something more than just the consensus of the moment, we have some very hard work to do to embody this more clearly. The next Lambeth Conference ought to address this matter directly and fully as part of its agenda.
>
> The reason Anglicanism is worth bothering with is because it has tried to find a way of being a Church that is neither tightly centralised nor just a loose federation of essentially independent bodies - a Church that is seeking to be a coherent family of communities meeting to hear the Bible read, to break bread and share wine as guests of Jesus Christ, and to celebrate a unity in worldwide mission and ministry. That is what the word 'Communion' means for Anglicans, and it is a vision that has taken clearer shape in many of our ecumenical dialogues.
>
> I make no secret of the fact that my commitment and conviction are given to the ideal of the Church Catholic.
>
> But what our Communion lacks is a set of adequately developed structures which is able to cope with the diversity of views that will inevitably arise in a world of rapid global communication and huge cultural variety.

> The tacit conventions between us need spelling out - not for the sake of some central mechanism of control but so that we have ways of being sure we're still talking the same language, aware of belonging to the one, holy, catholic and apostolic Church of Christ. It is becoming urgent to work at what adequate structures for decision-making might look like. We need ways of translating this underlying sacramental communion into a more effective institutional reality, so that we don't compromise or embarrass each other in ways that get in the way of our local and our universal mission, but learn how to share responsibility.

What the Anglican Communion does is of monumental ecclesiological importance for ecumenical dialogue. If the Anglican bonds of unity were loosened, if say the Anglican Communion became a type of federation of separate churches instead of a worldwide group united by a common prayer book, belief in the Apostle's and Nicene Creeds, in baptism and eucharist, with cross-national interlocking bishop, priest and lay leadership, defined teaching on discipline, and theological training, it would seriously jeopardize *ARCIC's* work. It would not really be clear what the Anglican Communion *was* and therefore with whom the Roman Catholic Church was talking, and for whom Anglican members of *ARCIC* were speaking.

It is fortunate to have Rowan Williams as the current Archbishop of Canterbury. As a clear thinking theologian, with a strong pastoral side, he makes plain that neither Western, liberal thinkers who often believe that society sets the agenda and the church must respond, nor the so-called global south, which asserts that it is the Bible that sets the agenda, represent classical Anglicanism. There is truth in both positions and Anglicans must not walk away.

> The difficulty of the Gospel is perhaps this: that it gives comfort neither to the legalist nor to the libertine. It doesn't say "You can win the grace of God by being good," and it doesn't say, "The grace of God makes no difference to you." It sweeps away the cobwebs and the veils, and makes us face a Jesus who says, So, do you need me or not? Are you hungry? Are you sick? Is your work, your life unfinished? Because if you are whole and not hungry, and finished, go.
>
> Rowan Williams, June 26, 2005

Extremely positive steps were taken in Rome on November 24, 2006. Benedict XVI and Archbishop Rowan Williams met and issued a Common Declaration. It noted the known problems, but focused on the progress. Most importantly, they announced the 2007 publication of *Growing Together in Unity and Mission*. This is the document from IARCCUM describes the theological agreements of the last forty years, and goes on to suggest and promote practical ideas that can be taken by both churches. This is a rather new platform to work from – more honest and direct. They were not afraid to speak of differences, yet they were utterly clear about the need for doable steps that can be taken together.

WINTER, 2007

Several important meetings, international and local, of different groups of Anglicans and their leaders took place early in 2007. To me they suggest that the conventional thinking is in flux, that the center is shifting, which augers well for the survival of the Anglican Communion and for ecumenical dialogue.

Firstly, contrary to popular predictions, when the top leaders, called primates, met in Dar es Salaam from February 15-19, Rowan Williams managed to keep everyone at the table, and they issued a unanimous communiqué at the end.

It asked hard things of the US, giving the Episcopal Church until September 30, 2007, to "make an unequivocal common covenant" that its bishops will not allow same-sex blessings in their churches and that it would not consent to the election and consecration of a bishop living in a same-sex union "unless some new consensus on this matter emerges" across the Anglican world. It also created a plan for temporary supplemental pastoral care for dissenting dioceses in the US.

Katharine Jefferts Schori has taken a measured, non-emotional yet pastoral stance. She has reported on the meetings and the different situations that each primate works in. She met with her Executive Council and they have convened a "work group" to consider what its role and responsibility is in this case. The US House of Bishops met in March. But I believe there will come a time when people will begin to understand the practice of a religion in a more subtle way, and be able to enter in and to participate in the quiet, the intellectual rigor, the depth and the complexity of the religious imagination, and the feelings of emotional release that the practice of a faith brings. Only then will we begin to . . .

Rowan Williams has met with the English Synod of Bishops, where dissent is even more pronounced than in the US, and warned against taking a prophetic stance if its one that no one can hear.

Things happen in dialogue and, to the surprise of many, there seems to be a growing and obstinate will to keep the Anglican Communion together, to use the existing structures to implement a more highly defined conciliar system of leadership. All of the churches have been asked to respond to a draft of a covenant that was presented in Dar es Salaam.

Much of the timetable revolves around the approaching Lambeth Conference, the once every ten year meeting of all the bishops which will be in June of 2008.

Deadlines and ultimatums can seem immutable at this moment of explosive growth of knowledge and worldwide changes but there can be surprising outcomes when committed and rational thinkers sit together.

LOCAL ANGLICAN / ROMAN CATHOLIC DIALOGUES, ACTIVITIES, IDEAS, AND CLASSES

There are pockets of ecumenical activity at the local level, from country to country. There is probably more knowledge of ecumenism in England than the US, but all Episcopal and Roman Catholic dioceses in the US have ecumenical officers. Joint activities tend to be most energetic where there is a natural affinity between local pastors, and overall since the attacks on the World Trade Center, more emphasis has been place on inter-religious dialogue.

The theological Anglican Roman Catholic dialogue in the US (*ARC-USA*) is strong and active. They meet twice a year and have been reflecting on the new document on Mary and will publish a parish resource text, called *Gift of Unity: A Study Guide for Episcopalians and Roman Catholics*. The guide studies the liturgical prayers of Baptism and Eucharist in each church.

There are numerous valuable books that offer prayers and services that can be used for joint worship. They are listed in an appendix.

In One Body Through the Cross, The Princeton Proposal for Christian Unity offers some valuable ideas for institutional exchange and activities.

> When full communion does not exist, churches should acknowledge and encourage special vocations for the sake of unity. God may call lay and ordained members of one church to sustained participation in the life and mission of separated churches, even if sacramental participation is not possible for a time.

Paragraphs 55-59, and 66 of the *Princeton Proposal* spell these ideas out. And places in Rome, such as the Anglican Centre, the Centro Pro Unione and Foyer Unitas, offer classes on ecumenism for lay and clergy.

> Ecumenical dialogue should not be undertaken only on the universal level; it must also become a duty at individual and local levels. It needs to be realized in each Christian's personal life when he or she meets Christians of other churches, in families, particularly mixed marriages, in local communities, in dioceses and at the level of Bishops' Conferences. Of particular importance is the ecumenical dialogue undertaken in theological faculties and institutes.
>
> Cardinal Walter Kasper, *That They May All be One, The Call to Unity Today,* 2004, p. 45

CONCLUSION

We've come a long way from spilling blood in Christ's name, but intense, atavistic memories persist, even when the overt polemics have died away. For some in the US, the pope is still a mythic, even dangerous figure. The potential for mutual suspicion is high in many places, sometimes particularly for active church members. That this conversation is so remote, so peculiar and so surprising to most people after forty years speaks volumes.

Clarification and reconciliation of doctrine had to be the important first step, but we can't get lost in the doctrinal bushes; theological discourse is obviously not an end in itself. This search will only have power and will only progress if it is part of a fuller story, part of the church's life and identity. If reunion were to magically happen today, it wouldn't hold and would be so peculiar as to frighten people.

We can't currently imagine what a re-statement of religious authority in the modern world would look like. *ARCIC's* work and the theologians have found language that shows that Anglican/Episcopalian and Roman Catholic doctrine often compliment each other. Desirous but mystified, this is a type of summons or call for something we can't quite picture.

Our secular leaders are bumping up against similar types of questions – what will be the most authentic and useful bonds and boundaries between the local and the universal in the years to come, between any community's local and immediate needs and those of all the world's people? What's the best relationship between the public good and private practices, the individual and the group? How will world leaders use laws of consent to establish basic human rights for all, but allow for individual conscience? How are we meant to live together in our individualized, but intensely networked and volatile world?

This confuses us today and is part of the reason for the ecclesiological identity crisis facing these two churches. We place an enormous emphasis on personal choice and on private conscience; it's hard for us to see the need for the universal, for the group. But when you get right down to it, individual freedom is meaningless in isolation. It only comes into play when we are in relationship and participate in the give and take of establishing the common good for all.

Finally, in a very practical way, who can help imagining the odd potential scenarios with a united Christendom – a Russian Orthodox at a Quaker Meeting, statues of Mary in Presbyterian Churches, prayers for a pope in a Pentecostal tent. Familiar habits of worship define and also comfort us.

But I believe there will come a time when people will begin to understand the practice of a religion in a more subtle way, and be able to enter in and to participate in the quiet, the intellectual rigor, the depth and the complexity of the religious imagination, and the feelings of emotional release that the practice of a faith brings. Only then will we begin to imagine a new reformation regarding the *nature* and *purpose* of church in our global world, giving it a new-found form and reality, that somehow will help people over the peculiar hurdles and doubts of our age.

And it is without doubt time to, in the meantime, emphasize and promote the *Lund Principle*, a concept developed in Sweden, way back in 1952, by the World Council of Churches.

> We should not do separately what we can do better or at least equally well together.

CHAPTER TEN

MY WORLD AND CHRISTIAN UNITY

Genuine ecumenical accomplishments, even after decades of determined work, have been elusive. Attempting to change the way people have thought and felt, for generations, about something as intricate and embedded as their religious beliefs is, and it should be, serious business. There has been progress though, and we've gotten beyond what English novelist Penelope Fitzgerald described happened in her family, when a great aunt converted to Catholicism.

> In later years she horrified her family by announcing that she and all her children were to be received as Roman Catholics. This meant that the sisters could never meet or communicate again, and both of them accepted this, in spite of the intense grief it caused. It was a division sharper than the sword.
>
> *The Knox Brothers,* p. 5

The Roman Catholic Church today is clearly committed to ecumenism and has articulated a broader ecumenical vision than ever before, and Archbishops Robert Runcie, George Carey and Rowan Williams have had bigger ecumenical dreams for the Anglican Communion than their predecessors. Importantly, some of Benedict XVI's first words have been about the importance of ecumenism. His first encyclical, *Deus Caritas Est*, (God Is Love) has established a creative and positive beginning. The leaders may not always know how to make progress, but there is one thing on which they all agree – *there is no going back.* It is the beginning of a new day.

But at the parish level, in many places in the United States, it has felt like a war among the Christian denominations, a war that the institutional churches appeared, at best, not to care about, and at times, to even promote.

*

The Reverend Mr. Punch, A. R. Mowbray & Co., London, 1960

Aug. 19, 1908   *Gunning King*

Parson (discovering odd-job man working at the chapel). 'Why, Giles, I was not aware that you cut the grass for the dissenters too?'

Giles. 'Well, your reverence, I does sometimes; but *I don't use the same scythe!*'

For us Americans to understand our relationship to the ecumenical movement and our thoughts about organized religion generally, it is helpful to set a larger context and to remember that it was, after all, the Protestant Reformation that drove our country's founding. The English Puritans and Pilgrims and others were driven by religious fervor, but they also emphatically sought freedom from *any type* of religious authority. America's founders wanted to be free to practice (or not) any religion they chose, but to be at the same time, free of any institutional religious power.

Young America wanted to create a government of laws, not of men, one that relied on reason to answer all questions. Hence, the United States eventually became the first constitutionally based country to form itself without an established religion.

> The only foundation left for a new order of peace was for the Christian religion to renounce its universal claim in the sphere of public life. It became a partial system, increasingly cast aside from the public sphere and confined to the private arena. This is the essence of modern secularization . . .
>
> Walter Kasper, *That They All May Be One, The Call to Unity Today,* p. 174

Scientific breakthroughs had begun to offer new ways of explaining the physical world and our relationship to it. We became the true Enlightenment test case baby, raised as described in the following passage, which defines Enlightenment thinkers:

> They shared a commitment to intellectual freedom, and a belief that tradition, especially religious authority, was an obstacle to human fulfillment. It is impossible to reduce their concerns to a formula, but the German philosopher Immanuel Kant (1724-1804) came closest to doing this successfully. In an article entitled "What is Enlightenment?" he answered: "Dare to know! Have courage to make use of your own understanding." Man's perennial immaturity, Kant continued, had been caused by his "lack of resolution and courage to use his understanding without the guidance of someone else."
>
> Isser Woloch, *Eighteenth Century Europe, Tradition and Progress, 1715-1789*, p. 231-2

This outlook has lead to several hundred years of unimaginable progress in deciphering the physical world and our biological make-up. That and the innovative growth of commerce and technology and the movement of capital have meant a better life for many throughout the world.

So today we are oriented, even hard-wired, toward an anti-authority religiosity, a belief in science and in the self over the group. The creation of unprecedented wealth has fostered this individual independence.

But we are also bumping up against and being discomfited by unexpected limitations. Not that much further ahead in eradicating poverty, racism, or evil than when we completely took things on faith, we're coming to realize that science, wealth and the social sciences will not be able to solve our most basic human problems by using reason only. They give us exciting but seemingly endless new chapters in a story with an unknown conclusion. These limits have created a dis-ease, and this disappoints us by reminding us of the inherent difficulty of explaining with certainty what distinguishes and underlies our lives.

> No technological achievements can mitigate the disappointment of modern man, his loneliness, his feelings of inferiority, and his fear of war, revolution and terror. Not only has our generation lost faith in Providence,

but also in man himself, in his institutions, and often in those who are nearest to him.

From Isaac Bashevis Singer, Nobel Lecture, December 10, 1978

*

The desire for freedom is not the property of one culture, it is the universal hope of human beings in every culture.

George W. Bush, *New York Times,* April 29, 2003

Is this true? If yes, why is it true?

John Rawls, the late philosophy professor at Harvard, asked the same question and toward the end of his life, came to wonder if it might be religious faith, of a certain sort, that was the very thing that rendered the desire and respect for human freedom rational. (John Rawls, *Lectures on the History of Moral Philosophy,* The Wilson Quarterly, 2000) The desire for freedom and for individual rights cannot be explained on purely autonomous grounds. They have to come from somewhere, and Rawls couldn't identify anything other than individual religious belief to describe how the drive for human freedom is activated and builds, from person to person.

Rawls' thinking parallels the most fundamental rock on which all Judeo-Christian creeds and beliefs are based. According to the *Hebrew Scriptures,* known more familiarly as the *Old Testament* to many Christians, each human being exists as a unique creation of God. As such, by birth, each takes a fully individual role in the dignity and the glory of the created universe, which at the same time unites person to person, and person to God. It is each person's individuality and this created commonality and relationship that call into existence the inherent human rights of every person. Once personal survival is secure, the desire for freedom emerges and grows.

*

Many people are genuinely confused today about what it means to practice a faith in our fast moving and plural world. Some have reacted to these disorienting changes by embracing fundamentalism, an answer-all solution that, carried to an extreme, obscurs all of the issues at hand. Many of us don't know how to answer the question "how much belief is enough," and by that I mean finding the balance between my autonomy and independence and my sacrificial obligations to the groups that I care about – family and friends country and church.

Most importantly, we don't understand what the global family of religions mean when each says that their teachings contain the full truth. This seems to deny the potential for the truth of my neighbor's faith. This rubbing together of diverse ideologies is the most difficult challenge facing all of the world's religious leaders and all thinking believers.

And Christianity is not about blind belief. It is just the opposite actually. It teaches that the formation of the self comes about by using free will to engage the intellect and the emotions. Then, since we don't live in isolation but in community, we engage with others who are doing the same thing. In this way, we examine the truths that the religions proclaim. It seems counter-intuitive, but most of us really only get to faith through a combination of experience and reason. It is the active and creative use of reason that leads us from thinking about ideas about God to actually experiencing God.

This route leads to doubt sometimes, and even disdain or indifference, but that is a normal part of practising faith. Christianity believes that only an honest and confident study of the well developed message of Christ will develop true believers, and teaches that, in the end, nothing can separate us from God's love.

> The freedom to seek the truth, and to confess it once it has been recognized, is therefore inalienable from a Christian point of view; it is a fundamental human right. The Christian faith can thus affirm its unconditional and universal claim to truth only in so far as it acknowledges and defends the freedom of all . . . So it does not have to surrender itself in a pluralist society; it can assert itself and at the same time affirm and defend the rights of all others who are seeking the truth.
>
> Cardinal Walter Kasper, *That They May All Be One, The Call to Unity Today*, p. 185

The actuality of religious differences and the characters and histories of many of the separate religions and denominations demonstrate the varieties of religious experiences. There must be ways to make use of the best of these developments and let the different ecclesiologies remain true to their histories, which can then contribute to enlivened ways of being together.

We know that the religion that most people practice is, generally speaking, an accident of where they were born. Furthermore, we see people from different religions fall in love with each other. What the church then is trying to say about religious truth is mightily complex and has to be very carefully expressed.

And most unfortunately, people sometimes just tune out to what the churches are saying because their experiences of them are so different from the official pronouncements.

*

While not accurate, Roman Catholics and Anglicans are typically stereotyped as having very different ways of thinking about church and about their relationships to it. Anglican (and Protestant) faith is commonly described as being more private and personal, and having a more intense relationship with the Bible, *sola scriptura*, whereas Roman Catholics historically claim a more intense experience of the mystery, or as Hans Urs von Balthazar called it, the 'indwelling,' which is centered in the regular sharing of the Eucharist.

> Luther could no longer share that certainty which recognizes in the Church a community consciousness superior to private reflection and interpretation. Thus the relationship between the Church and the individual, between the church and the Bible, is fundamentally altered. This is the point that the Congregation [Congregation for the Doctrine of the Faith] would have to pursue with Luther if he were alive, or rather, this is the point, which, in the ecumenical conversations, we do discuss with him. This question is also naturally at the root of most of our conversations with Catholic theologians.

Cardinal Joseph Ratzinger in Vittorio Messori's, *The Ratzinger Report*, p. 158

It is not coincidental that Luther's focus on the importance of Scripture reading for everyone happened simultaneously with the phenomenal opportunities created by the printing press. In Anglican England, the link-up between church and state that the printing press offered was even more intense.

Maybe originally Martin Luther sought a more personal, direct connection to God and maybe Roman Catholic theology has relied more on Greek philosophy and metaphysics, but there actually exists a huge range of acceptable beliefs and practices within each church. Further, among scholars within the same church, there is much discussion and disagreement, even about doctrine. Theological exploration, development, and challenge thrive in the scholarly journals, from both Roman Catholic and Anglican churches, and close fraternal relations exist among church leaders, clergy and theologians across the denominations.

The Roman Catholic Church does try to keep dissent *within the family* and it has famously reined in certain academics and clergy who afterward, it is interesting to note, generally chose to stay in their church and live with the censure. The hierarchy sends mixed signals to Roman Catholic politicians, but for a church of 1.3 billion people, it allows quite a lot of scope. Cardinal William Levada, the new President of the Congregation for the Doctrine of the Faith, explains it this way:

> But a theologian himself or herself is called to discriminate between where that inquiry leads and how it corresponds to the faith that the Church continues to receive and live by. Otherwise they would not be doing true theology, it seems to me. Theology itself is in dialogue with revelation, which has some things to say. And you can't just say that revelation says anything you want it to say.
>
> *The Tablet*, June 11, 2005

There also remains, for some in the Roman Catholic Church, a strong and separate self-identity and a moral superiority, exemplified in this answer from Stephen Daedalus in James Joyce's *A Portrait of the Artist as a Young Man*, when he is asked if he has become a Protestant. "I said that I had lost the faith, but not that I had lost self-respect." (Page 238)

The residual anti-Catholic bias in our collective unconscious also needs to be acknowledged as there exists an embedded strain of anti-Catholicism that is hard for the United States to shake, and it goes back to our country's founding.

> It was in the twentieth century that the distinguished historian Arthur Schlesinger said that the deepest bias in the American people is the anti-Catholic bias.
>
> John R. Quinn, *The Reform of the Papacy*, p. 55

This bias, which used to run along class and ethnic lines, now views the church's social teachings, as exemplified in the anti-birth control teachings of the 1968 encyclical *Humanae Vitae*, and its stance against gay marriage and any number of life and death issues, as an inappropriate overreaching into an individual's privacy and basic human rights.

While the sometimes justifiable frustration with the Roman Catholic hierarchy is more widespread in Europe, especially in Germany, than in the United States, the discovery that some bishops in the American church protected pedophile priests disturbs and shocks us, and is still being studied and absorbed.

Official Roman Catholic stances exacerbate the way that some former Roman Catholics see their ex-church. For many of my friends, the flame of faith was doused early on through experiences of theological rigidity in parochial schools and under the thumb of the local church. At a young age many American Catholics closed down, and either lost any desire for, or ability to, believe at all or found their religious homes elsewhere.

But today's over-simplifications of the two faiths represent the poles and diminish both faiths, contributing to unchallenged and accepted misunderstandings that serve to keep us in camps. To make matters worse, certain tendencies in the media see only the extreme or odd cases and the problems as being newsworthy. This unintentionally distorts the potential for dialogue, because there is no accurate popular picture of actual ordinary day-to-day life in the churches. Most believers don't live at the poles; it is our ordinary, everyday lives that we treasure the most. If people understood this and these two churches better, they'd be more open to exploring ideas about unity.

Titanic events such as the 9/11 attacks in the US and the international terrorist bombings of the last few years tie us more vitally to the larger issues, and create a renewed desire for connections to others – family, culture, government, military, church. Life's seriousness bores down into the imagination and the whole world sways, as we absorb the blows. We've become motivated to solving the lesser problems because the huge international ones have jolted us and connected us to a very complex and possibly de-stabilizing and dangerous future.

In spite of or maybe because of the fact that it was a religious movement that drove the founding of the United States, we are conflicted about talking about religion and very sensitive about discussing matters of personal faith. Yes, there are some prominent leaders whose evangelical beliefs are well known, but, in general, among educated Americans, to talk about a committed life of faith creates discomfort and it is a questionable topic.

Polls tell us that we Americans believe in God, but somehow, it feels so un American to talk about it or to openly submit ourselves to the rigor involved in a commitment to belief. We have incredible power, but reluctance to enter into, and to say yes to something we can't *know*.

For the English, and to a lesser extent the Europeans, while they may not exhibit such overt belief, they do believe in the fundamental *existence* of the church, be it established or not. Personal and church and state histories are thoroughly entwined. "There will always be a church." We have no deep memories of when the church persecuted and was itself victimized. We Americans, because of our Puritan heritage, tend to think of religion more personally, and less corporately, whereas for Europeans, the former entanglements of the religious and the political, remind them of old non-theological wars. Some in the US may see the Church as irrelevant. Some in Europe see it as dangerous. A popular current option is to see religion as just another value-neutral 'ism' in identity politics.

I am not suggesting any model, but the political and international orders are in flux. The post-modern, post-Christian, post-denomina-tional era is ending. You know you're in the middle of something new when people who define themselves as atheists are declining as fast as those who define themselves as church members. The issue is no longer about belief or unbelief. It is about indifference. "Maybe there is a god, but whether there is or not, has nothing to do with me."

The period without a name is fading and our perception of what reli-gion is, or can be, is changing also. Viewing any strong religious experi-ence as mindless or intellectually weak, and any serious religious belief as being superstitious or hypocritical, is just beginning to give way. Future innovative church relationships will provide a bridge between what has become an intensely self-conscious moment, which has logi-cally grown out of Enlightenment ideas of each person's uniqueness, and an unimaginable future.

One thing I think is becoming clear: we cannot understand ourselves by ourselves and reason alone does not suffice. Belief in something greater than ourselves is what unites us and underpins how we live, how we express ourselves, and how we delve into the possibilities of the transcendent, the wholly other, or the Old One, as Albert Einstein named God. After all, pondering the ultimate questions is what has underlied the creation of art and thought in the West.

The comprehensiveness of the religious imagination gives us the ability to understand our complex world in a freer, and a more expansive and intuitive way. We have had a fear of faith and believing because it has seemed so irrational to believe, so un-American to accept the self-submis-sion required by faith. But faith and religious precepts are of a different realm, and religious faith cannot just be explained; it can only be experi-enced. The common traditions of the different religions build on observa-tions of human nature and create a faith to draw on, even when they have trouble explaining this to the culture. The days of religion being able to successfully claim a blind allegiance or unquestioned authority are over. As I've said before, honest, real religious truths will only take root and grow when knowledge, experience and reason come to life.

*

Reformed relations in the Christian churches will not come along in conventional or expected ways. The split between Rome and Canterbury arose for jurisdictional reasons and only after the fact did the dispute become about doctrine, which then slowly came to be accepted church teachings. We now have had doctrinal momentum for near to forty years, but not much real institutional will, and certainly very little local knowledge, of the search for unity.

We don't know how to imagine a different future time yet, but even with the internal problems of the churches, no one is going back. Ecumenism is not political accommodating. Its radical, ahead of its time paradigm-shifting thinking is the Holy Spirit at work in a world that finds itself increasingly interdependent.

Anyone can see that it is a white-hot moment of dissension, confusion and change in the world's religions. When people are ready for a new and as yet unknown way, it will flare up and appear, and, just as in the aftermath of Martin Luther's scrupulosity, it will catch fire and the world will be different.

Though sometimes mystified about how to move forward, no problem is so formidable as to preclude dialogue. Christ's prayer "May they all be one" remains. Seeking oneness is not an optional extra, but rather learning and receiving from each other is a divine imperative. Ecumenism *is* the future of Christianity.

Proceed, with caution. But proceed.

EPILOGUE

t has taken me a long time to realize that the real genesis of this book was not a summer course at the Anglican Centre in Rome in 1998. It is rooted, rather, in my childhood.

I am the oldest of five, with a faithful Catholic mother and a father not so interested in religion, though his mother was an active Presbyterian. We lived in the San Joaquin Valley, the broad, hot farmland of central California, and attended a nearby Catholic grammar school.

One day, I came home from school and told my mother that I had learned that people who were not Catholic were not going to go to heaven, and, therefore, I wanted to know, what about Dad? She stopped whatever she was doing, and we walked back to school. My mother politely told Sister Stellita Marie that as James Sorensen's wife, she believed she knew better than sister did about whether or not he was going to go to heaven. She knew something about his morals and the nature of his conscience, and she believed that, based on the life that he was living, it was very likely that he would be sharing heaven with his family.

From that, I learned two essential faith, and life, lessons: one, that only God can know or understand each person's eternal relationship with him, and, two, that a developed faith and examined conscience require that you speak up, even before the stated authority of the church.

More importantly, in the whole of my Catholic upbringing and schooling, I was embedded with a reality that has guided and sustained me in all ways throughout my life. It is the belief that God is present in me and in every person, not predominantly as a shield or as a judge, but as a life-giving and pleasurable mystery and, at times, as a powerful source of support. It is an ever-running two-way current, the comfort and challenge of which is incomparable.

A COMMON HISTORY: CHRISTIANITY'S EARLIEST DAYS

Christianity was birthed in the Middle East, at the most western end of Asia, just where Europe and Africa meet. The area could be called the religious cradle of the world, since more than half of today's population claims their religious heritage to this tight small area.

Two thousand years after Christianity's founding, some 2,600 different groups call themselves Christian, and claim a direct connection with the teachings of the New Testament. They are everywhere around the globe, and account for more than one third of the world's population. They have responsibility for over 50% of the world's resources.

*

The first Christians were mainly Jews, who spoke Greek, and lived in and around Jerusalem, the central city of the most recently conquered flank of the Roman Empire. Roman power had superceded Greek dominance by the time of Jesus' birth, and the Roman Empire comprised much of the world that was known to the Romans, which was centered in the Middle East and Europe, obviously a very small portion of the whole world. Roman administrators allowed Jews religious freedom, and though the language of Jesus of Nazareth was Aramaic, a Palestinian dialect of Hebrew, educated and traveled citizens spoke Greek.

This southeastern area of the Mediterranean was an important geographical, commercial and philosophical center. The major Influences of the Ancient and Classical worlds were present here, as were significant numbers of people. It is estimated that the total world population was about 200 million at this time, and several hundred thousand lived in and around Jerusalem. Egyptian, Jewish, Greek and Roman ideas and cultures interacted and cross-blended.

The earliest movement outward of the first Christian believers was to the north and to the west of Jerusalem, and into Asia Minor (today's Turkey), Cyprus and Greece, to Samaria, Damascus, and Antioch, which was a capitol city of the Roman Empire. One of many competing Jewish sects, the early Christians struggled among themselves with what they believed, with what would be included in the official writings, and with differing ideas on how to organize themselves.

SOME CHRISTIAN COMMUNITIES BEFORE A.D. 70

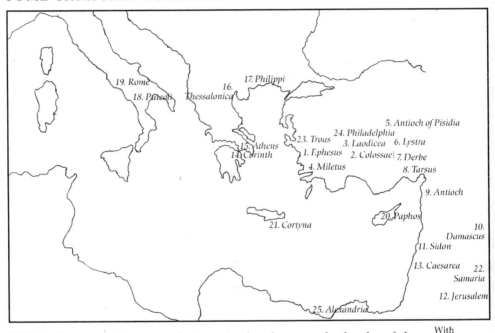

Within the competing texts that survived to become the books of the gospels, which were written from about 60-100 and codified by about 200, there are several stories that describe these controversies. Generally, Peter and James, two of the apostles, in their letters and books, attempt to restrict membership to other Jews, but Paul, in his letters to the people of Galatia, Ephesus, and Corinth, argues clearly and dramatically for inclusiveness, which establishes an unmistakable idea and sets a specific path for the development of Christian orthodoxy and doctrine.

Of course, there are many reasons for the success of the early Christian movement. The members were active proselytizers and, since Jews

With acknowledgment to W.H.C. Frend and *Peters Compact World Atlas,* Hammond World Atlas Corporation, Union, NJ 2002 were already spread throughout the Mediterranean, there was a dispersed base to begin with. Also important to Christian success was the often misunderstood doctrine of forgiveness which is not just the "simplistic notion of indiscriminately turning the other cheek, [it] actually proves to be part of a complex, context-dependent system of responses ranging from forgiveness to retaliation." This is thinking that serves to produce a future advantage.*

*Jared Diamond, *New York Review of Books,* November 7, 2002, p. 30

They couldn't have had the remotest thought that these beliefs would be developed, translated and spread so broadly, that the very marking of years on the calendar, used by the whole world, would eventually be ordered around the birth date of Jesus of Nazareth.

From the Greek comes the word eucharistia, which means thanksgiving. And, probably, from Greek habits, came the idea of the partaking of a sacred communal meal. This simple act of sharing the Eucharist, the communal exchange of the bread and the wine, the physical substances of life, gave and gives today cause and connection to the life of each Christian who partakes of it. It is human beings, of all backgrounds, together participating in the most essential and life-sustaining and celebratory event in daily life.

The beauty and symbolism of this simple act of sharing food at a table, with anyone who chooses to be baptized, and remembering the significance of who and what has come before and looking to whom will follow, makes strangers kin and powers the heartbeat of the Christian church.

The Roman Emperor Constantine, in 313, was the first to officially sanction Christianity, which he did with the *Edict of Milan.* While Constantine had been in Italy, attempting to consolidate the eastern and western flanks of the Roman Empire, a mystical vision of a cross had led to his conversion. At that time, the Eastern branch of the Roman Empire was wealthier and more developed and dynamic, and at the center of the world's population. Constantine established Christianity as the religion of the empire, and in 330, 240 years before the birth of Mohammed, he celebrated his creation, Constantinople, today's Istanbul, the city he intended to become the center of the Christian world. On the same latitude as Rome, Constantinople grew quickly to a population of about 20,000. Constantine was specifically attempting to create distance from the less developed, more chaotic West, from Rome and from Arles, which had been other possible building centers for him. Constantinople because the Eastern center, and a counterpart to Rome, that was by nature more Hellenistic, and partially accounts for the early and ever-present distinctions that existed, and would build, between the Christian churches of the East and of the West.

It was from Constantinople that Constantine called the bishops together to address some of the controversies that were building in this juvenile church. This innovation was the first attempt in history at a world-wide meeting of dispersed religious leaders.

Held in Nicea, today's Iznik, in northeastern Turkey in 325, the meeting was huge for its day, though only four or five Western bishops attended. About 300 bishops were there, and they voted for the first draft of a creed, a version of which continues to be a fundamental church document for Christians. It had been first used in about 180, in Rome, for baptisms. Some of the ideas in it would need to be more precisely defined however, because from the very beginning it meant different things to different people.

This general meeting was large-scale 'work by committee' - bishops came with the ideas of their people at home, and knew that whatever they agreed upon at Nicea would have to work at home. This council began the cycle of church-wide ecumenical (from Greek, meaning world-wide) meetings that were called to deal with the uncertainties and disagreements in the growing church, and with the inevitable questions raised by growth, by the difficulties of melding different cultures from spread out regions, and with the passage of time.

Opened, paid for and possibly chaired by Emperor Constantine, and lasting over the summer months, the meetings in Nicea didn't completely solve the first big controversy of the young church, which was introduced by Arius, a priest from Alexandria. Arius believed that Jesus was more man than God, and therefore a lesser being than God. Not surprisingly, the complex and primary belief that Jesus was both God and man would need clarification after the *Council of Nicea*, along with the sophisticated idea of the Trinity. What exactly did it mean that there were three persons in one, and that Jesus Christ was both God and man at the same time?

The Father and the Son had been declared to be of one substance and the same, but this construction and the language of Nicea, which was developed to correct Arius and his followers, were ambiguous and open to interpretation. Clear writing and thinking by Athanasius (300-373) of Alexandria, and others solved the problem and described the fragile balance between "the threeness and the oneness in God, (and) gave full meaning to the classic summary of Trinitarian doctrine, three persons in one essence."*

*Timothy Ware, *The Orthodox Church*, p. 23

These assuaging and inventive words of Athanasius calmed the situation, but the contrariety and differing emphases between the East and the West did not go away.

The early Christian Church was active in Africa, which was the theological powerhouse of the time, especially in the patriarchal city of Alexandria. Tertullian (160-225) and Cyprian of Carthage (200-258) set the foundation for major doctrines, including original sin and the Trinity, and St. Augustine, (354-430) born in Algeria, today's Souk Ahras, lived and wrote in northern Africa. The first monastic (from the Greek word monazein, meaning to be alone) order was founded in Africa by St. Anthony, rather unbelievably reported to have lived from about 251-356. Over eighty Christian monasteries were established along the Nile between 300 and 700.

The other early councils were called and led by the emperors, or the Eastern patriarchs, and were held in the Eastern world, with the emperors taking an active role in promulgating the decrees. The last one, in 787 in Nicea again, settled the icon controversy by ruling that icons would be allowed in church. Since God had become man, it was justifiable to portray a human-like image of him; they represented a kinship between God and the viewer. Icons were to enhance prayer, not to be worshipped.

The decisions arrived at at the first councils were rooted as much in guiding, as in pronouncing. This seems inevitable considering the diversity of voices and locales represented, and because these clarifications were often so rooted in the ineffable.

The councils confronted the difficult questions that were brought from the various regions, and a working principle was that they would last as long as was needed to achieve unanimity or near unanimity in the decrees they passed. They referred often to the earliest sources to assist their thinking. The early contentions of Arius and others were helpful because they forced debate and discussion and helped the early church to clarify their teachings, which ultimately produced clearer, more creative thinking.

As the population expanded out from the center of the Eastern church in Constantinople, there were conflicts, related to teachings, style and jurisdiction. The four ancient patriarchal sees of the East - Constantinople, Alexandria, Antioch and Jerusalem – had only needed to be focused on the church. It is important to note that their patriarchs and bishops were never secular leaders, in the way that the bishop of Rome was.

The church in the East therefore had never had to be as much *in the world* as the church in the West was. The East was a more cohesive and unified world, and the Byzantine emperor controlled the secular scene. Europe, on the other hand, was undeveloped, with feuding and warring chieftains, and the patriarch of Rome was an important and powerful figure, secularly as well as spiritually. He came to serve as an anchor, and as a center of stability and unity for much of the European continent.

As this situation evolved, the person of the pope became a centralized center of authority, which was not the case in the East. Because there were four patriarchs, power in the Eastern Church was always more diffused and had to be more conciliar. They were used to decision-making by committee. To illustrate this, Russia, which was converted to Christianity beginning in the late 900's, uses the same word, sobor, for church as it does for council.

They intensely resented the non-conciliar alteration to the Nicene Creed that was made at the Third Council of Toledo in 589. The phrase *and the Son* was added to the Nicene Creed, which then read "who proceeds from the Father and the Son." The phrase is called the Filioque, and it was probably developed and inserted to make crystal clear the son's equality with the father and as a device to refute the lingering ideas of Arius. For practical and theological reasons, it was always strongly opposed by the Orthodox Church.

> From the start, Greeks and Latins had each approached the Christian Mystery in their own way. At the risk of oversimplification, it can be said that the Latin approach was more practical, the Greek more speculative; Latin thought was influenced by juridical ideas, by the concept of Roman law, while the Greeks understood theology in the context of worship and in the light of the Holy Liturgy. When thinking about the Trinity, Latins started with the unity of the Godhead, Greeks with the threeness of the persons; when reflecting on the Crucifixion, Latins thought primarily of Christ the Victim, Greek of Christ the Victor; Latins talked more of redemption, Greeks of deification; and so on.
>
> Timothy Ware, *The Orthodox Church*, p. 48

Because the Eastern and Western regions of the Holy Roman Empire grew and developed such different strains of Christianity, the mutual excommunication that came in 1054 surprised no one. Though 1054 may be a somewhat arbitrary date, the separation was real and it arrived after centuries of distrust, of differing experiences and liturgy, and of language and geographic separation. Eastern Christians also had the pressure of the burgeoning Muslim world, which was growing rapidly.

Today there are about 220 million Orthodox Christians, compared to over one billion Roman Catholics, with about 7 million Orthodox Christians living in the United States. Orthodox priests are free to marry, but bishops must be celibate, and are mainly from the monastic orders. Divorce and remarriage are tolerated, up to three times, though the ceremony is supposed to be different after the first marriage. Governance is actually more akin to that of the Anglican Communion, though there is more uniformity regarding teaching and morals.

The patriarch of Constantinople, who is called the Ecumenical Patriarch, holds a primacy of honor. The extended system of churches, many of which are organized along different political boundaries, are either autonomous, which means that they are connected to one of the original four patriarchates, or they are autocephalous, meaning that they are churches organized by political boundaries and are not under the jurisdiction of one of the original patriarchal sees. They have maintained a uniform doctrine and liturgical practice.

In December of 1965, Athenagoras and Pope Paul VI, met in Rome, and officially nullified the anathemas from 1054, thereby inaugurating the beginning of a complex dialogue that has worked on theological questions.

The relationship between Rome and some of the Orthodox churches was made more hopeful, but also more complex with the fall of the Berlin Wall.

AGREED *ARCIC* DOCUMENTS

Eucharist (1971) · Ordination (1973) · Salvation and the Church (1986) · Church As Communion (1991)

EUCHARIST: AGREED STATEMENT 1971

In my Catholic growing up and schooling, I was taught that in the Mass, at the time of the Consecration, the bread and wine became *in fact* the body and blood of Jesus Christ. The mysterious and medieval word transubstantiation described this transformation, and one had to believe this in order to be a faithful Catholic.

This was a fact. Period. Transubstantiation was the term used to communicate the mystery; this framework for understanding the Eucharist was probably based on an early concept from St. Ambrose of Milan (about 340-397), and became official only in 1215 at the Fourth Lateran Council. It was rationally non-sensible, from any number of points of view, but it was fundamental to what a Catholic believed. And, perhaps as importantly, we were taught that it was something that Protestants (we didn't know what Anglicans were) did not believe.

The Eucharist was the first subject that *ARCIC* tackled and they intentionally did not use the word transubstantiation in their final agreed statement, except in a footnote. This was not just being polite; they were following the instructions laid out by Pope Paul VI and Archbishop Michael Ramsey and trying to get *behind* the language that had contributed to the divisions. By using all the available scholarship, old and new, they were trying to help people to break out of habits and assumptions. This also had the possibility of making the meaning of the Eucharist freshly potent and clear, in a way that was accessible for both churches.

They focused on the purpose and on the meaning of the Eucharist, rather than attempting to describe how it worked. There were two key theological concepts they needed to resolve: the understanding of the Eucharist as sacrifice and the term 'real presence.'

The Consecration of the Eucharist is *not* a small drama offered to the people by the priest. It is a real-time moment of recalling for today and now Christ's one-time sacrifice of his death on the cross. Through Holy Communion, the congregation and the celebrant together share in the benefits and the mystery of Christ's once-for-all sacrifice and in the on-going existence of Christ in the world for each person from the past, in the present and for the future.

This conception of Eucharistic meaning does not diminish the uniqueness or the perfection of Christ's one time propitiatory act on the cross; rather, this understanding of the Eucharist passionately *ties us* to his unrepeatable sacrifice. This is what communion is and means, and *ARCIC* used a biblical word, the Greek word anamnesis, "the making effective in the present of an event in the past," to describe with certitude that Christ was present sacramentally and substantially for both Anglican/Episcopalians and Roman Catholics.

The very nature and purpose of the Eucharist is an intimate and personal union or exchange. "Thus, in considering the mystery of the Eucharistic presence, we must recognize both the sacramental sign of Christ's presence and the personal relationship between Christ and the faithful which arises from that presence." (Paragraph 8)

They also reached the conclusion that for both churches, belief in the real presence of Christ at the Eucharist, another way of expressing a significant piece of the meaning of transubstantiation, is embedded in the core doctrines of both churches and forms the center and essence of their liturgies. Christ's exhortation, "*You* do *this* . . ." (Luke 22:19) creates the on-going tie between his presence and the lives of his believers.

> It is a sign, needing to be grasped and thought about. Catholic teaching is clear. Christ is not physically present in the same way that other people and objects are present, but he is sacramentally present. His presence, in other words, is not corporeal or dimensional. So for instance, when the host is broken, Christ is not broken.
>
> Alban McCoy, *The Tablet*, October 22, 2005, p. 16

Paragraph Six of the *Elucidations of the Eucharist and Ministry* (1979) tries to answer concerns that were raised in some of the responses to the 1971 agreed statement.

> It does not imply that this becoming follows the physical laws of this world. What is here affirmed is a sacramental presence in which God uses the realities of this world to convey the realities of the new creation: bread for this life becomes the bread of eternal life.

Most people have not been pondering transubstantiation and *ARCIC* documents, but the Eucharistic liturgies of the two churches have in quite a natural way grown to be very similar over the years and today are practically identical in language and form. (I was in Cambridge, Massachusetts at the Cowley Brothers monastery with a German friend, who assumed that we were in a Roman Catholic Church up until the intercessory prayers, when the congregation prayed for Bishop Barbara.) While there are still some Episcopal parishes in the United States where Sunday liturgy continues to be predominately Morning Prayer, this is becoming the exception and throughout the Anglican Communion there continues to be an organic evolution toward the weekly, and sometimes daily, celebration of the Eucharist.

ARCIC's work did not exhaust what could be said about the subject of the Eucharist, and there are some in both churches who would disagree with some of the language used or not used. But for *ARCIC* members and most Anglican and Roman Catholic worshippers, the meaning of the Eucharist is clear. Its meaning is understood by faith, and is experienced and nurtured weekly at the Eucharist. It unites the present with the past and the future. It is for everyone, it is for forever, and, according to *ARCIC* theologians, its meaning is the same for both Roman Catholics and Anglicans.

MINISTRY AND ORDINATION: AGREED STATEMENT 1973

Everyone knows that there are different official disciplinary practices regarding the priesthood within each church, which for Roman Catholics means that their priesthood is male and celibate. For Anglicans, priests are permitted to marry; in some provinces, women can be ordained; and, controversially, certain dioceses have ordained practicing homosexuals. That these differing disciplinary or moral practices have been more sharply drawn in the last thirty years is perishingly difficult for the Anglican Communion especially and has complicated the dialogue. However, *ARCIC's* brief was not to deal with contemporary ethics or disciplinary practices, but rather with the *origin and nature* of ministry and ordination.

ARCIC examined whether or not there was agreement in the answers to the following three primary questions about ordination:

1) Is ordination a sacrament, as both churches conceive of the word sacrament?

2) Has there been an unbroken line of priests, consecrated by bishops that date back to apostolic times?

3) What is the nature of priesthood, especially as it relates to the Eucharist?

ARCIC agreed that Christ originated the priesthood, that we have received it as a gift of the spirit that comes through the church and that it has three orders. There is the unique priesthood of Christ, the priesthood of all believers, and thirdly, the priesthood of the ordained minister. *ARCIC's* document is concerned with the ordained priesthood, which follows a direct line back to the apostles and is of a different order than that of Christ or of the priesthood of all believers. An essential responsibility of the ordained ministry is oversight (episcope). *ARCIC* affirmed that only someone who was ordained can officiate at the consecration of the bread and wine and that ordination is a sacrament for both churches, in spite of the fact that the 1552 Anglican ordinal had not referred to ordination as a sacrament.

They were very aware of the 1896 papal pronouncement that had said that 'Anglican orders were absolutely null and utterly void,' and devoted time to understanding that decision and how it had been made.

Since the ARCIC agreed document on ordination was issued, in 1973, several events have created a new context for the exploration of *Ministry and Ordination*. In 1978, the Vatican Archives from the 1896 period were opened and the documents from the actual discussions about Anglican Orders have been studied. The released documents show that there was not unanimous agreement within the committee that made the decision and that the pronouncement was not intended to end the discussion or the relationship with Anglicans.*

Additionally, Pope Paul VI had, in 1968 and 1972, reformed and simplified Roman Catholic ordination rites, which had the unintended result of blurring the former distinctions with Anglican ordinations.

Cardinal Johannes Willebrands, at the time the head of the *Pontifical Council for Promoting Christian Unity*, stated in 1985 that in light of the 'new context,' referring to the liturgical renewal in both churches, the opening of the documents and ARCIC's clarifying work, the papal bull from 1896 would have a basis on which to be re-evaluated.

This all went a long way to answering the first two questions, but what about the crucial third one – what are the requirements of the priestly nature as it relates to the Eucharist especially? Must priests be male? Celibate? Heterosexual?

The discussion of Ordination became more complicated beginning in 1974 when the Episcopal Church in the United States became the first of the Anglican Provinces to begin to ordain women regularly. In its 1979 *Elucidations*, ARCIC said that "it believes that the principles upon which its doctrinal agreement rests are not affected by such ordinations; for it was concerned with the origin and the nature of the ordained ministry and not with the question of who can or cannot be ordained." (Paragraph 5)

Today, the ordination of women as deacons and priests is widespread throughout the Anglican Communion. There are only six of the 37 provinces that do not ordain women, and there are three dioceses in the US that do not. After twenty-five years of dialogue about the subject and the practical experience of women serving as priests and, in the United States and a few other areas, as bishops, leading parishes and dioceses, it has become second nature, where once it hadn't seemed

*R. William Franklin and George Tavard, *Journal of Ecumenical Studies*, p. 261-286

clear that it fell within acceptable theological bounds. The spiritual life of the Anglican Communion has been enlivened because of it, and for many, many Anglicans it does not represent a theological change, but rather a development in the ordering of the ministry.

Somewhere between 75-100 formerly Anglican/Episcopal priests are now Roman Catholic priests in the United States because, in good conscience, they couldn't stay in a church that ordained women. Many of these former Anglican priests were married, and they and their wives and children form a tiny and anomalous part the Roman Catholic family, as do the married priests from the Eastern-rite churches which are in full communion with Rome.*

Milwaukee Journal Sentinel, September 5, 2003

But it has been a confusing stumbling block that certain Anglican provinces ordained women without the approval of the Lambeth Conference, as the 1988 letter from John Paul II to Archbishop Runcie makes clear. Both the fact that certain provinces would make this decision *on their own* and the decision itself "appears to preempt this study and effectively block the path to the mutual recognition of ministries."**

**Common Witness to the Gospel, p. 21*

Answering questions about what one's *nature* has to be in order to be suitable for the priesthood was not part of *ARCIC's* original brief and both churches are in the middle of wrestling with this internally, though most Roman Catholic theologians would agree that a celibate priesthood for Roman Catholics is a disciplinary choice and not a theological necessity. Even back at the Malines Conversations in the 1920's, the concept of a married priesthood was not a problem.

> Roman documents have always clearly stated that celibacy was a disciplinary practice of Roman Catholics and not essential to the offices of the ministerial priesthood.***

***Laurentio B. Guillot, Ministry in Ecumenical Perspective, p. 108*

Churches are not immune to evolving cultural mores that put pressure on them to re-order their disciplines. Much of the stresses in churches today revolve around questions related to human sexuality and are related, in my opinion, to consequences of the fallout of women being able to determine when or whether to have children. The disconnection between sex and procreation is a direct outcome of the invention of the birth control pill. This and the associated changes cannot be over-looked or waited out. They've initiated too fundamental a re-ordering.

> If we as Anglicans and Roman Catholic Christian leaders cannot speak with conviction, credibility and true guidance about issues of human sexuality and about the roles of men and women in church and society, we are condemning the next generation to a do-it-yourself values wilderness in which the blind mislead the blind.
>
> J. Dick, The Malines Conversations Revisited, p. 79

In 1991, the Vatican finally responded to the 1973 agreed statement on *Ministry and Ordination*. They described the document as being not so much wrong, as less than full. Many specific questions were posed and to many whose hopes had been raised, the document read like a cold blast. One area that the Vatican specifically addressed regarded the important third question, the *character* of the priest. Since Jesus Christ was male, the Vatican response was that all future priests would have to be also.

Several of the national Anglican/Roman Catholic dialogues responded also.

The French Roman Catholic Episcopal Commission for Christian Unity's response to the Holy See's response asserted that they were "astonished at the demands for an identity of formulations in an age when we live in a society which has become conscious of its multicul-tural character."* The French Roman Catholic bishops also pointed out that "one cannot insist that the views expressed will be identical with the formulations of councils which took place after the separation without any participation on the Anglican side."**

The Anglican/Roman Catholic Consultation in the United States (ARC-USA) in 1992 responded to the Lambeth and Vatican responses to *ARCIC I*. ARC-USA saw the *Final Report of ARCIC* as "both resource and agenda in the Anglican-Roman Catholic relationship. Together with the responses to it, the *Final Report* clarifies certain questions and poses certain challenges that seem to mark where the next steps must be taken in our journey together." (Paragraph 15) It noted that while the acceptance

*C. Hill & E. Yarnold, *The Search for Unity*, p. 173

**C. Hill & E. Yarnold, *The Search for Unity*, p. 174

of it from the bishops at the *Lambeth Conference* of 1998 was important, it was a problem that because of the nature of Anglican governance, "their response is not a legislative or juridical decision. (Paragraph 35) And in Paragraph 17 it noted that the Vatican Response seemed to create an unreasonable and impossible burden by requiring *ARCIC* I to produce language that was "identical with traditional Roman Catholic theological formulations."

The *ARC-USA* response makes two other useful observations that are related, one general and one specific. It points out some of the difficulties inherent in expressing what is *the faith of the church*. The problem to which it points is that the words of official doctrinal and liturgical formulae, as well as faith statements of any individual or community, all fall short of the mysteries that they seek to express. At best, when Christians seek to articulate the faith of the Church, we deal with degrees of inadequacy. (Paragraph 27)

In a 1994 letter to the Co-Chairs of *ARCIC II*, Cardinal Edward I. Cassidy, the President of the Pontifical Council for Promoting Christian Unity, said that "no further study would seem to be required at this stage."

> I was able to confirm officially that no further work needed to be done on the presentation of Anglican and Catholic faith in the Eucharist. It was possible to state also that there was agreement on the nature of ministry in the church, although the question of the person of the minister able to celebrate the Eucharist remained unsolved.
>
> Edward Idris Cardinal Cassidy, *Ecumenism and Interreligious Dialogue*, p. 56

*

In 1986 and 1994, *ARCIC II* published two documents that explained the common ground that exists in the two churches with regard to two doctrines that shape Christian life – justification and salvation. These documents explain the interaction between God's grace, that is given completely unconditionally and bountifully, and how a person chooses to receive this grace within the context of the local and the universal church.

SALVATION AND THE CHURCH: AGREED STATEMENT 1986

God's grace acquits one of any sin and also, most importantly, offers an 'intimate and personal relationship,' that has to be 'freely grasped and accepted,' in order for the individual to be transformed and to demonstrate this transformation in the world. A material related theme is what role the church in the world should play in leading a person to the fullest understanding of this mutual action.

A Catholic response to the *Agreed Statement on Salvation in the Church*, which came from the (Vatican) *Congregation of the Doctrine of the Faith*, laid out, point by point, the theological concerns that the document raised, and in summary determined that the official Vatican response could not "affirm full and substantial agreement . . . primarily because of deficiencies concerning the role of the church in salvation."* This referred to the teaching role reserved for the pope.

Common Witness to the Gospel, p. 50

In a more general way, it also accused the commission of not creating adequately rigorous doctrinal formulations; it complained of 'reciprocal compromises' and argued that the

> symbolic nature of the language makes difficult, if not impossible, a truly univocal agreement where, as is the case here, questions are treated which are decisive from the dogmatic point of view and figure among the historically most controversial articles of faith.**

**Common Witness to the Gospel, p. 50*

The *Congregation of the Doctrine of the Faith*, headed by Cardinal Joseph Ratzinger, was saying that by using symbolic language instead of dogmatic language, *ARCIC* had intentionally sidestepped certain important issues.

A response from the Anglican/Roman Catholic Dialogue of Canada pointed out that the thinking of the *Congregation of the Doctrine of the Faith* was "not easy to square with the traditional theological view that statements about God and the things of God are not univocal but analogical . . . Mystery will never be exhausted by language." It further said that this fact need not lead to "imprecision."

This exchange touches on a key theme in the *ARCIC* discussions, which is that of the ever-present difficulty of finding language that can accurately express the depth of an ancient and complicated theology, and that can also place it in a context that is fresh and intelligible to the current age. Faithful, effective ecumenism plays a role in the continual restating of theology, because it is always aware of the fact that attempts to express the mystery of God and his grace, will, by definition, be incomplete.

THE LOCAL AND THE UNIVERSAL:
AGREED STATEMENT ON *CHURCH AS COMMUNION* 1991

This agreed statement centers on the considerable connection and collaboration that exists already between these two churches and tries to bring all of the earlier agreed documents together by explaining the ecclesiology behind them. This consolidating document does not concern itself solely with doctrine; its purpose is to explain the real but imperfect communion that exists already, though this is more or less true in the differing regions of these two churches.

The document talks about the relationship of the local, where most of us experience the church, to the universal. In Paragraph 39, it says that

> Life in self-sufficient isolation, which rejects the enrichment coming from other local churches as well as the sharing with them of gifts and resources, spiritual as well as material, is the denial of its very being.

And in Paragraph 27:

> Consequently in every age and culture authentic faithfulness is expressed in new ways and by fresh insights through which the understanding of the apostolic preaching is enriched. Thus the Gospel is not transmitted solely as a text. The living word of God, together with the spirit, communicates God's invitation to communion to the whole of his world in every age.

It balances this appreciation of the responsibility of the local with an understanding that both churches have bishops whose role it is to keep the church united in a common faith.

> This ministry of oversight has both collegial and primatial dimensions . . .
> It is exercised so that unity and communion are expressed, preserved, and fostered at every level – locally, regionally and universally. In the

[115

context of the communion of all the Churches the episcopal ministry of a universal primate finds its role as the visible focus of unity.

Paragraph 45

While popular perceptions of one another are often distorted, sometimes willfully, and while there have been divergent patterns of authority, there has been extraordinary organic convergence in liturgy, social outreach, shared space and in collaboration on educational materials for adults and children. That a respected children's education series, the *Catechesis of the Good Shepherd,* is used and highly regarded by both Anglican and Roman Catholic parishes in the United States speaks volumes, and may yield unintended consequences.

The *Common Declaration* of 1989 of John Paul II and Archbishop Runcie emphasized the commonality between the two churches and urged the faithful and the clergy to recognize and cherish the "certain yet imperfect communion we already share . . . The ecumenical journey is not only about the removal of obstacles but also about the sharing of gifts." And, finally, the ecumenical imperative exists " not only for the credibility of the church's witness and for the effectiveness of its mission, but supremely for the glorification of the Father." (Paragraph 23)

MORALS: AGREED STATEMENT ON TEACHINGS AND PRACTICES (1994)

We know of course how penetratingly difficult the subject of morals is today. The world is alive with faithful people whose beliefs in this area are diametrically opposed, and who feel that they have no place to meet. And, as usual, there is sometimes closer agreement across the different denominations than there is within each denomination. But we must remember that just as the world is perpetually in flux so are the churches, and the study of doctrine is meant to help and support people but it cannot, indeed should not, be separated from how a life of faith is actually lived.

In this agreed statement, the first of all of the post-Vatican II ecumenical dialogues to address morals, *ARCIC* does three things.

- · Firstly, they give a thoughtful and developed over-view of the underlying and relevant moral and spiritual theology of both churches.
- · Secondly, they explain the differences that have evolved regarding how the leadership and the laity interact as related to morals.
- · And, thirdly, they explore the actual official teachings that are specifically different, and those where ambiguity exists.

It is popularly assumed that there are extensive differences in the moral teachings of the two churches, but following their familiar pattern, *ARCIC* made no assumptions, and set about to identify the convergences and the differences.

They assert that the continuing 'breach of communion exacerbates the moral life of all Christians,' because with the Christians in a cold war, the church's message and effectiveness is compromised and subliminally weakened. This implicitly poses the question of whether the continued separation is actually creating more serious problems, than would exist if the relationship could be mended.

THE THEOLOGICAL OVER-VIEW

While one wants to rush into the facts, the document wisely slows us down and starts by reminding us that all life is relational, interdependent and communal, and that true personhood has its origin and roots in the mutual exchange of love between God and the people of his creation. Therefore, each person has the responsibility to exercise that God-given free will in the expression of each's absolutely unique one-of-a-kind personhood, and also, as importantly, in support of the common good.

The shared common assumptions that flow from this original foundation inform and direct both communions. Every single person has a part to play in discerning how he or she will live in the world. Each person, informed by that individuality and by the teaching and tradition of the community, struggles for goodness and renewal. The church, for its part, strives to understand the best way to help to develop each individual conscience and each person's moral compass, and it also determines the best way to "reconcile and support those members of the communion who have, for *whatever* reason, failed to live up to its moral demands."

CHURCH ORDER, LEADERSHIP AND LAITY

Roman Catholics and Anglicans have developed different ways of supporting people in the living out of a life and also differing ways of responding to those who are not living up to the teachings. Also, the role of authority, or the teaching voice of the church, in the formation of moral judgment, is different. A few words on church organization will help here.

Originally, for Anglicans, the practice of their religion was much bound up in the life and culture of England. Parliament played a strong role in the life of the church, and therefore the lay voice always had a clear place and a great weight in church leadership. As the Anglican Church branched out around the world, the newly formed churches in each country developed local styles and systems of governance. In the United States, after the Revolutionary War, when it became clear that there was not going to be an established religion for the new country or for any state, Anglicans came together and gave significant power to the laity by determining that their bishops would be elected by a vote that included both clergy and lay, and since their ecclesial structure continued the line of apostolic succession, they named themselves the Protestant Episcopal Church of the United States of America.

The churches of the Anglican Communion are grouped today by provinces, and the leaders of these 39 provinces meet together every other year. All bishops in the Anglican Communion, about 750, meet every ten years to make decisions that express the "mind of the communion" on issues that will affect the whole communion. These decisions "have a high degree of authority, but they do not become the official teaching of the individual provinces until they have formally ratified by each of them."

The center of operations for the Roman Catholic Church is Vatican City, which is itself the smallest state in the world, comprising about 108 acres, and of which the pope is the sovereign. Since Vatican II, the Roman Catholic laity has had more of a voice and it is a more important one than it used to be, but it is specifically an advisory one. For Roman Catholics, the bishops, with the bishop of Rome (the pope) as the leader, have the duty of establishing and interpreting their church's teachings and governance.

It may surprise Anglicans/Episcopalians to learn that there always has been and continues to be a wide range of accepted orthodoxy within Roman Catholicism, though, in recent years, there has been a push toward reining in theologians in certain fields. There are a few famous cases of the silencing of particular voices, but the Roman Catholic Church is too big and too practical to not allow quite a lot of freedom,

SOME VITAL STATISTICS

ANGLICAN COMMUNION

Description
Worldwide group of provinces in communion with the See of Canterbury and each other. United by a common history derived from the Church of England, with common traditions of uniform prayerbook, doctrine, discipline and worship.

History
Because it was an island, England was never as totally integrated into the Catholic Church as European countries were. Became the established church in England during the reign of Henry VIII's daughter, Elizabeth I. It was saved from becoming a small insular sect during the English move toward Empire and by the Evangelical, Tractarian and Broad Church movements of the 1700's and 1800's.

Iconic identity
From the beginning, known for finding a middle way (the via media) between Roman Catholicism and Protestantism. Fosters and depends on an active lay role in leadershipc

Top Leader
Rowan Williams, 104th Archbishop of Canterbury decides, with the Anglican Consultative Council and the primates, who is invited to the Lambeth Conference. He is the appellate authority in certain circumstances.
He has the right to crown the Kings and Queens of England.

Top leader in USA
Katharine Jefferts Schori, Presiding Bishop as of November 4, 2006.
First woman elected to lead a province.

International Governance
Without a hierarchical structure, the following groups are in place to govern the whole communion:.
Lambeth Conference – Begun in 1868, and held every 10 years; all of the bishops meet in England
The Anglican Consultative Council, composed of 2-3 members from each province and meets every year.
Biannual Primates meetings, leaders of the 38 provinces worldwide. See page 65.

Proposed changesh
Use of a covenant, to be signed by each province, is being explored as a way to bind together the disparate provinces.

Average Anglican, in demographic terms
An African female, under thirty mother of 3, lives on less than $1.50 a day, and is related to someone with AIDS

Cultural and social mores
Anglicans divorce and practice birth control at about the same rates as Roman Catholics.

Adherents
Worldwide	USA
77,000,000	2,300,000

Distinguishing characteristics
Universal use of the Book of Common Prayer - part breviary, part missal and taken from ancient Roman Catholic and Orthodox liturgies with Lutheran influence also.

Ecumenical Involvement
On-going national and international dialogues with the major Christian bodies and the world's religions

Current issues
This is a pivotal moment of public wrestling about authority and church order, reflective of unresolved tensions about the role of faith in a global culture and in individual life.

SOURCES: Anglican Cycle of Prayer, The Anglican Communion Office, ACC, 2005?%Arthur M. Allchin, The Witness of the Anglican Communion & A. E. J. Rawlinson, Anglican History and Beliefs
Anglican Communion Website

ROMAN CATHOLIC CHURCH

Description
Its headquarters is the world's smallest nation, Vatican City, which is within the city of Rome. It has the largest number of adherents of any religious body.
It is a 2000 year history of unity achieved through councils, adaptation, retrenchment, and an ultimate practicality.

Iconic identity
Oldest voluntary group of people, unified internationally through the leadership of the pope.

Top Leader
Pope Benedict XVI
As a head of state, the pope is briefed every morning, and there are full diplomatic relations with 174 countries.

Governance
Re-organized by Sixtus V in 1588 , the Curia is the world's oldest governing body.
About 2600 clergy and laity work in a system of dozens of congregations, councils, and academies – from the Doctrine of the Faith, to the Pastoral Care of Migrants and Itinerant People, to the Causes of Saints, to the Pontifical Academy of Social Services, to the Councils on Inter-religious Dialogue and Promoting Christian Unity, to name a few.

Adherents
Worldwide	USA
1.1 billion	658 million

Ecumenical and inter-religious work
On-going national and international dialogues with the major Christian bodies and also with the world's religions

Particular challenges
Defining what the church is most essentially – a holy mystery or the community of believers? When/if to disenage priesthood and celibacy, and related questions in the sexual sphere.
Distinguishing between heresy and legitimate dissent and judging when to issue censures.

Cultural and social mores
Roman Catholics divorce and practice birth control at about the same rates as Anglicans. American Catholics receive the large majority (80%) of anullments.

Average Roman Catholic or Anglican, in demographic terms
An African female, under thirty, mother of 3, who lives on less than $1.50 a day, and is related to someone with AIDS

Distinguishing Characteristics
Name the ideal, and then provide infinite compassion and pastoral concern for those who do not live up to it.

SOURCES: Pontifical Yearbook, 2005
Adherents.com
Vatican website

though that is obviously not at all its reputation.

So how do both churches believe the nurturing and development of moral judgment is best taught and ordered today, especially given their histories? Clearly, Anglicans believe the moral life is best developed and supported by a dispersed authority, by local bishops and pastors; Roman Catholics, on the other hand, believe in the need for a central authority to "preserve unity and to give clear and binding teaching." They both agree that all "moral authority is grounded in the goodness and the will of God," and that authority and liberty are two sides of the same coin.

The perceived ways of working and the caricatures of the two churches are only half-truths. "It is not true that Anglicans are pragmatic and unprincipled, while Roman Catholic moral theology is principled but abstract. It is not true that Roman Catholics are always more careful of the institution in their concern for the common good, while Anglican moral teaching is more utilitarian."

An important difference historically has been the differing beliefs about how the distinctions between canon law and moral law should be interpreted. For Roman Catholics, canon law "with its incorporation of contingent and prudential consideration" has some leeway for pastoral concerns, but moral law, on the other hand, is absolute and universal. Anglicans, on the other hand, believe that *in certain situations*, even moral law needs a more nuanced interpretation and that "it might be right to incorporate contextual and pastoral considerations in the formulation of moral law." (Paragraph 52) Anglicans believe this because they believe it is more respectful of individual conscience and liberty and also that it is a wiser and more effective way to foster obedience to the most essential moral values. Some Roman Catholic theologians would see no differences between Anglicans and Catholics at the level at which they make their decisions and live their moral lives.

Anglicans also believe that, in some cases, the life in faith is jeopardized without this flexibility. Perhaps it is akin to the way a parent evaluates the differing needs of each individual child, or as St. Benedict wrote in his rule for life in a monastery, written in the early 500's, "He [the abbot] must know what a difficult and demanding burden he has undertaken: directing souls and serving a variety of temperaments, coaxing, reproving and encouraging them as appropriate."* The abbot has the job of knowing who to sharply chastise and who to be gentle with, to bring to full life, what is within each monk.

The Rule of St. Benedict, Chapter 2, Sentence 31

After setting up this background, *ARCIC* observed that there are two areas where church teachings have officially diverged. One is on marriage after divorce, during the lifetime of a former spouse, and the second is on the permissible methods of controlling contraception.

Again, *ARCIC* said that before exploring the points of disagreement, it was important to explain the mutual foundations from which differences have grown.

MARRIAGE AND DIVORCE

Human sexuality reveals God's most profound creation at work. Sexuality endows human beings with the capacity for communication at the deepest level. "It is ordered toward the gift of self and the creation of life." (Paragraph 55) It needs to be integrated into an ordered pattern of life, and it founders when it becomes the occasion for sexual self-centeredness.

> Both our traditions treat of human sexuality in the context of the common good, and marriage and family life as institutions divinely appointed for human well-being and happiness. (Paragraph 58)

> Marriage is not merely a commitment with life-long obligations; it is a vocation to holiness.

> *Lambeth Conference*, 1958, Resolution 112

However, for both Roman Catholics and Anglicans, this life-long commitment to the marriage is not always possible. Human frailty enters and the binding love that existed is broken down. How can the vows and the sacramentality of the union be respected, but severed? Can a sacrament be voided?

Both churches seek to be obedient to Christ's teachings, but interpret differently what is called for. At the beginnings of Anglicanism, Anglicans chose to keep the familiar Roman Catholic teachings on divorce and remarriage, and not to follow the Protestant reformers who allowed divorce, on the grounds of adultery or desertion. In England, it wasn't until 1857 that divorce and the freedom to marry again was available to Anglicans in general, though the second marriage was not allowed in a church; before 1857, divorce in England was only for the rich and influential, and it happened only through an Act of Parliament.

As Anglicanism spread and the dispersed churches began to take their places in the worldwide Anglican Communion, each made its own marriage discipline based on local custom and law.

The *Lambeth Conference* of 1978 reaffirmed the 'first-order principle' of life-long union, but it also acknowledged a responsibility for those for whom marriage as a life-long union may be available was not possible.

> The Anglican position, though equally concerned with the sacramentality of marriage and the common good of the community, does not necessarily understand these in the same way. Some Anglicans attend more closely to the actual character of the relationship between husband and wife. Where a relationship of mutual love and trust has clearly ceased to exist, and there is not practical possibility of remaking it, the bond itself, they argue has also ceased to exist. When the past has been forgiven and healed, a new covenant and bond may in good faith be made.
>
> Paragraph 75

Both churches have sought to find the right balance in understanding the sacramentality of marriage, but also to recognize the fact that human beings err and enter into marriages where the love and the bond is lost. "Roman Catholic teaching and law uphold the indissolubility of the marriage covenant, even when the human relationship of love and trust has ceased to exist and there is no practical possibility of recreating it."

Today, most, but not all, Anglican provinces allow, after careful pastoral consultation, for a marriage after a divorce, to be solemnized in church. The local bishop determines what type of ceremony or blessing is appropriate to each circumstance. This is akin to the practices of Orthodox Christians, who also allow remarriage after divorce.

For Roman Catholics, the history of these matters is "long and complex" (Paragraph 69), and the *Code of Canon Law* of 1917 attempted to clarify very old practices that were based on the teachings and practical practices of St. Paul and St. Peter. Marriages could be dissolved if one of the parties was not baptized or a fully committed Christian, and marriages that were not between two baptized persons were not considered to be sacramental and hence could be dissolved. Anglicans had never made these distinctions.

> In the period following the breach of communion, the Roman Catholic Church continued to uphold the doctrine of indissolubility reaffirmed at Trent. At the same time it developed a complex system of jurisprudence and discipline to meet its diverse practical and pastoral needs and to provide a supportive role for those whose faith was threatened by a destructive marital relationship. (Paragraph 67)

How the spiritual and physical bonds that exist together in a marriage work is a mystery. St. Augustine in the 5th century saw this and used a passage from the *New Testament*, from *Ephesians 5:32*, to describe the 'ontological permanence' that he perceived to be embedded in the marriage vows.

Just as relationships between countries, families, friends and, as we have seen, even churches, break down, so too with marriages. Anglicans and Roman Catholics agree that marriage is sacramental, but they do not agree on what this fact means and this affects their practices regarding divorce. Does an indelible mark remain that some how should keep a divorced person from receiving the Eucharist?

Baptism is not erased when faith falls away; what should be done when the love that held the marriage together has vanished and nothing can repair it? Roman Catholic teaching is not trying to be difficult here. It is simply convinced that if a marriage contract between two baptized persons was entered into with full and free consent, and the marriage was duly consummated, it cannot be dissolved by any human authority.

Today, especially in the United States, Roman Catholics who wish to remarry after a divorce often chose to obtain an annulment. An annulment, which was actually what Henry VIII was looking for, is a statement that asserts that the marriage had never been valid, due to some defect or some essential element that was missing when the marriage vows were exchanged. Though Roman Catholics in the United States account for only about 6% of all Roman Catholics worldwide, they receive about 80% of the annulments.

Annulments, which are unique to Roman Catholics, are often used when a couple wishes to remarry in the church. They can be very blunt and sometimes painful instruments, however, because their language requires the couple to declare that their marriage had never been valid, even after years of marriage and the raising of children.

Roman Catholics and Episcopalians divorce at about the same rates, but divorce is actually an instrument of the state, not the church, and the Anglican/Episcopal Church, unlike the annulment offered by the Roman Catholic Church, has no liturgy to dissolve the marriage bonds.

> On the level of law and policy, neither the Roman Catholic or the Anglican practice regarding divorce is free from real or apparent anomalies and ambiguities. While therefore, there are differences between us concerning marriage after divorce, to isolate those differences from this context of far-reaching agreement and to make them into an insuperable barrier would be a serious and sorry misrepresentation of the true situation.
>
> Paragraph 77

It is an extremely confusing topic. How can official Roman Catholic teaching allow a person, who, hypothetically, has murdered a spouse, to confess and then to continue to receive communion? And to even remarry, while divorced persons who remarry cannot receive communion? Why can a laicized priest, someone who has received the sacrament of ordination, continue to receive communion? These contradictions make it seem as if the sacraments were weighted differently and it creates a difficult, perplexing and painful situation for many, many people.

Communion after divorce is a hot and lively topic, especially in Germany, one of the most liberal areas of the Roman Catholic Church. In 1994, the *Congregation for the Doctrine of the Faith* (CDF) and a group of German bishops exchanged a group of public letters. The German bishops desired permission to allow divorced and remarried Catholics 'to approach holy communion when they consider themselves authorized [by] a judgment of conscience to do so,' and that a priest could 'respect [this] decision in conscience to approach holy communion, without this implying an official authorization.'* This was impossible, according to the *CDF*, because the reception of communion, like a marriage, was an 'inherently public reality.'

*Weigel, George, *Witness to Hope*, p. 941

> The theological gravamen was the spousal nature of the Church: to be divorced-and-remarried was to be living in a situation that contradicted, objectively, the indissoluble union of love between Christ and his Church which is signified and effected by the Eucharist. To admit the divorced-and-remarried to communion would be to concede that marriages could be dissolved: that seemed to suggest that the love of Christ for the Church could be dissolved.
>
> George Weigel, *Witness to Hope*, p. 941

This seemed to controvert something that Benedict XVI had written in 1972, where he cited St. Basil to support allowing divorced and civilly remarried Roman Catholics to receive Holy Communion, under certain circumstances.

> In a 1972 essay reflecting on the council, Ratzinger argued for allowing divorced and civilly remarried Catholics under some circumstances to receive the Eucharist. He cited St. Basil: "There it is stated that after a longer penance, Communion can be given to a digamus (someone living in a second marriage), without the suspension of the second marriage; this in confidence of God's mercy who does not leave penance without an answer. . . . It seems that the granting of full communion, after a time of probation, is nothing less than just, and is in full harmony with our ecclesial traditions.
>
> *National Catholic Reporter*, John Allen, October 4, 2002

In his 1997 book, *Salt of The Earth*, Pope Benedict, then Cardinal Ratzinger clarifies his prior thinking by saying that questions of morals should not be solved legally, but rather at the pastoral level.

> There, he proposed that, while the principles remained unchangeable, 'experienced pastors' could perhaps make an 'extrajudicial determination that the first marriage did not exist.'
>
> Joseph Ratzinger, *Salt of the Earth*, p. 207

Groups of German bishops have continued to agitate, and to share communion with divorced parishioners and, at times, defiantly, with Protestants.

CONTRACEPTION

Procreation is one of the divinely intended joys of marriage and 'God calls married couples to responsible parenthood.' Having said this, both churches believe that 'there are some circumstances in which it would be morally irresponsible' to have children. There is not agreement, however, about the methods by which this decision, and these responsibilities, should be exercised.

Before 1930, both churches would have counseled abstinence for couples who had a justifiable reason to avoid conception. The *Lambeth Conference* of that year made a change, in Resolution 15, and said that

> where there is a clearly felt moral obligation to limit or avoid parenthood, and where there is a morally sound reason for avoiding complete abstinence . . . other methods may be used.

Pope Pius XI's encyclical, *Casti Connubii,* in 1930, answered the Anglican bishops and reaffirmed the traditional Roman Catholic forbidding of contraception, and this position has been often reaffirmed ever since, most recently in 2005.

Roman Catholic teaching sees the two essentials of marriage - loving union and procreation - as inseparable, and therefore each and every act of sexual intercourse must be open to procreation. This is fully discussed in Pope VI's encyclical of 1968, *Humanae Vitae.*

Many Roman Catholics have found a practical middle way between church teachings against contraception, and having each act be open to a pregnancy by choosing to have sexual relations only at the times when the woman is not fertile, informally called the rhythm method. As methods of determining when to abstain from sexual relations have become more scientifically sophisticated and exact, questions are raised of whether the rhythm method is actually a form of contraception.

But the lived experiences of the Roman Catholic laity educate them as much as their church teachings and many find themselves seriously at odds with church's teachings on birth control. The wedge that this issue has introduced for the people, their pastors and many theologians has created a problematic dynamic. The ban on any type of artificial birth control means that for many people who approach the communion rail, there is an inner tension, both for them and for their pastors. How many in the magisterium really believe that so many of the faithful, the priests, and theologians are wrong and not living up to church teachings on this issue? Again, in *Salt of the Earth*, Cardinal Ratzinger seeks a personal and pastoral, and not legal or canonical, solution.

> I would say that those are questions that ought to be discussed with one's spiritual director, with one's priest, because they can't be projected into the abstract. Joseph Ratzinger, *Salt of the Earth*, p. 203

For Anglicans, the integrity of the married relationship as a whole is the most important reality. It cannot be parsed and broken down into separate acts, sexual or otherwise.

*

There are two other areas where the official teachings on morals of the two churches are not officially defined as being different, those regarding the practice of abortion and relations between homosexuals.

ABORTION

> Anglicans have no agreed teaching concerning the precise moment from which the new human life developing in the womb is to be given the full protection due to a human person. Roman Catholic teaching, on the other hand, is that the human embryo must be treated as a human person from the moment of conception. For Roman Catholics, the rejection of abortion is an example of an absolute prohibition. For Anglicans, however, such an absolute and categorical prohibition would not be typical of their moral reasoning.
>
> Paragraphs 85 and 86

In the United States, the argument has been rigidly and, in the legal sense, quite crudely drawn. There is little room for reasonable and faithful people to talk about the moral difficulty inherent in examining and understanding when life begins, and discussing any appropriate limits on abortion.

> Archbishop of Canterbury Rowan Williams has written about his concerns about abortion and some of the inconsistencies present in the debate, especially when framing the discussion in terms of "choice." Choice implies relationship and exchange. We can't, on the one hand, claim that a fetus is meaningless and unidentifiable, and then proceed to discourage the pregnant woman from smoking . . . when we make recommendations about exercise or lifestyle. from *Lost Icons*, 2000

This type of thinking could be helpful in trying to enlarge this discussion.

HOMOSEXUALITY

> Both [churches] affirm that a faithful and lifelong marriage between a man and a woman provides the normative context for a fully sexual relationship. Both reject, therefore, the claim sometimes made, that homosexual relationships and married relationships are morally equivalent, and equally capable of expressing the right ordering and expression of the sexual drive.
>
> Paragraph 87

Here again, different approaches to the formulation of law and ecclesiology are relevant. While not castigating homosexual persons, Roman Catholic teaching holds that all homosexual activity is 'intrinsically disordered,' and concludes that it is always objectively wrong. This affects the kind of pastoral advice that is given to homosexual persons. Anglicans could agree that a homosexual life is a diminished one, but "there may well be differences among them in the consequent moral and pastoral advice they would think it right to offer to those seeking their counsel and direction." (Paragraph 87)

As we have seen with the pastoral dimension of advice to divorced persons receiving Holy Communion, it is likely that privately there is more leeway in the counseling and advice given to homosexuals.

The election of an openly gay man to be the Episcopal bishop of New Hampshire in August of 2003, has created a storm of internal dissension for the Anglican Communion, and difficulties for its dialogue partners. The story took the place in the US, at least temporarily, of the human sexuality abuse and cover-up stories of the Roman Catholic Church. It will take some time for the Anglican Communion to absorb what this will mean for it and the outcome is not clear. (There is more written about this in Chapter Nine).

ARCIC's document, which came out in 1994, claims that these differences are not fundamental, and need to be weighed in the larger context.

> The urgency of the times and the perplexity of the human condition demand that they [these two churches] now do all they can to come together to provide a common witness and guidance for the well-being of human kind and the good of the whole creation. Paragraph 88

CONCLUSIONS

Both churches are active worldwide, and have sought the best ways to promote the world's welfare, and to help people to live a seeker's life, one that fuses the day-to-day life decisions of the world, with larger eternal demands.

> The widespread assumption, therefore, that differences of teaching on certain particular moral issues signify an irreconcilable divergence of understanding, and therefore present an Insurmountable obstacle to shared witness, needs to be countered. Even on those particular issues where disagreement exists, Anglicans and Roman Catholics, we shall argue, share a common perspective and acknowledge the same underlying values. This being so, we question whether the limited disagreement, serious as it is, is itself sufficient to justify a continuing breach of communion.
>
> Paragraph 1

The document closes by calling for more working together, especially locally, to study the values that are shared, and to promote a global "perception of fundamental human relationships and values." Paragraph 100

APPENDIX IV

MARY: GRACE AND HOPE IN CHRIST

This document on Mary concludes this phase of *ARCIC*. Cardinal Walter Kasper, President of the *Pontifical Council for Promoting Christian Unity*, asked for the following when the new *ARCIC* agreed statement on Mary was made public last May.

> What is needed now is a wide-ranging reflection on the document itself so that Anglicans and Catholics alike may feel drawn to conclude that the document 'expresses our common faith about the one who, of all believers, is closest to our Lord and Saviour Jesus Christ.'
>
> Paragraph 1, cf Paragraph 63

It is safe to say that few, if any, of the topics that *ARCIC* has addressed have remained static and unchanged since the original breach, let alone since *ARCIC* began their doctrinal examinations in 1969. Both churches' teachings and practices have shifted over the years, growing more similar or apart, as focus, emphasis, and shades of meaning have been influenced by human experience and the changing needs of the church. "The freedom to respond in fresh ways in the face of new challenges is what enables the Church to be faithful to the Tradition which it carries forward." (Paragraph 3) Good ecumenical work integrates value from different periods and approaches, as it addresses the range of practices that have developed over time.

This may be nowhere more apparent than in the teachings and beliefs about Mary. She is a complicated figure by definition. She is the mother of Christ, a figure who is both God and man. She was born without sin, yet is fully human. There is no avoiding the importance of understanding her and her unique role. "Her response was not made without profound questioning, and it issued in a life of joy intermingled with sorrow, taking her even to the foot of her son's cross." (Paragraph 5)

ARCIC took a chronological approach in writing this document and began by looking at scripture, and the ancient common traditions, including the early church writers and councils. They then moved on and studied how Mary was thought of during Medieval Times, and then chronicled the subsequent developments in each church.

Finally, they used this information to under gird their examination of what can be said is really at the heart of the matter – the two papal definitions on Mary, from 1854 (*Immaculate Conception*) and from 1950 (the *Assumption*). Or, more, precisely, they addressed Anglican concerns about whether these dogmas/teachings grow out of scripture or are pronouncements without clear scriptural basis.

SCRIPTURE AND EARLY WRITINGS

The gospels of Matthew, Luke and John all describe Mary.

> Matthew emphasizes the continuity of Jesus Christ with Israel's messianic expectations and the newness that comes with birth - the birth of the Saviour. Descent from David by whatever route, and birth at the ancestral royal city, disclose the first. The virginal conception discloses the second.
>
> Paragraph 13

In Luke, where she represents the fundamental inwardness of faith, the inevitability of suffering, and the human capacity to continue to grow in understanding, she is "in a unique way the recipient of God's election and grace." Also in Luke, in the annunciation, which recapitulates several incidents in the *Old Testament*, Mary is the favored one, which implies that her holiness was pre-existing.

> Belief in the virginal conception is an early Christian tradition adopted and developed independently by Matthew and Luke. For Christian believers, it is an eloquent sign of the divine sonship of Christ and of new life throughout the Spirit. The virginal birth also points to the new birth of every Christian, as an adopted child of God. Each is "born again (from above) by water and the Spirit" (John 3:3-5). Seen in this light, the virginal conception, far from being an isolated miracle, is a powerful expression of what the Church believes about her Lord, and about our salvation.
>
> Paragraph18

Mary, by her roles in John's gospel, at the wedding at Cana and at the foot of the cross, displays not just motherliness, but also as "the one closest to Him who never deserted him, the object of Jesus' love, and the ever-faithful witness." (Paragraph 26)

The *Athanasian Creed* (date and author unknown) declared that Christ was "man of the substance of his mother." She defined and anchored his humanity, which sets her at the center of Christianity's belief that Christ was both God and man.

Augustine had this to say about Mary and her state of fullest grace, or sinlessness. (Paragraph 38)

> We must except the holy Virgin Mary, concerning whom I wish to raise no question when it touches the subject of sins, out of honor to the Lord; from him we know what abundance of grace for overcoming sin in every particular was conferred on her who had the merit to conceive and bear him who undoubtedly had no sin.
>
> *De nature et gratia* 36.42

Her title Theotokos, a Greek word that means God-bearer, was formally invoked at the *Council of Ephesus* (431) in order to help safeguard teachings on the unity of Christ's person.

ANCIENT COMMON TRADITIONS

So early councils slowly came to praise Mary, and her identity and role was established, especially in the East, by the fourth century.

Churches began to be devoted to her and there were feasts in her honor, some mirroring the commemorations of the events of the life of the Lord. December 8 was celebrated as her conception and August 15 as her dormition. (Dormition is the word used in the East and assumption is used in the West.) These were based on scripture and on early "legendary narratives" of the end of her life.

> Belief in her assumption was grounded in the promise of the resurrection of the dead and the recognition of Mary's dignity as Theotokos and Ever Virgin coupled with the conviction that she who had borne Life should be association to her Son's victory over death, and with the glorification of his body, the Church.
>
> Paragraph 40

There was a lot of discussion of her in the high middle ages – Aquinas and Duns Scotus "were deployed in extended controversy over whether Mary was immaculate from the first moment of her conception." (Paragraph 42)

Exaggerated devotions to Mary were disapproved of by Thomas More and Erasmus and were an issue for the English reformers, though they, and Martin Luther also, accepted that Mary was "Ever Virgin." (Paragraph 45)

It was her significant popularity that contributed to the decision to issue the1854 papal dogma on her *Immaculate Conception*, and likewise the 1950 one on her *Assumption*. (Paragraph 47) This devotion to her was somewhat tamped down at Vatican II, and one is now set within the context of Scripture and ancient tradition.

THE PAPAL DEFINITIONS

> We agree that nothing can be required to be believed as an article of faith unless it is revealed by God. The question arises for Anglicans, however, as to whether these doctrines concerning Mary are revealed by God in a way which must be held by believers as a matter of faith.
>
> Paragraph 60

And we once again come to the crux of this issue. Do the papal dogmas on Mary purely reflect scripture or has something been added or modified? Their out-moded language does not help the situation, and this agreement notes that they need to be re-received, in both churches, in the language of today.

MARY IN THE LIFE OF THE CHURCH

The image *ARCIC* sets in the paragraph 64 is especially strong.

> The Scriptures portray Mary as growing in her relationship with Christ: his sharing of her natural family (*Luke 2:39*) was transcended in her sharing of his eschatological family, those upon whom the Spirit is poured out (*Acts 1:14, 2:1-4*).

This visceral expression of her role enlivens how Anglican and Roman Catholics have interpreted her. Roman Catholics have tended to ask for her intercession and help, using the prayer the *Hail Mary*, whereas Anglicans have seen her as a "model of discipleship." She has a distinctive and significant place in both churches, and individual, regional and cultural diversity is evident and appropriate.

ARCIC concludes this document with the following paragraph.

> Our statement has sought not to clear away all possible problems, but to deepen our common understanding to the point where remaining diversities of devotional practice may be received as the varied work of the spirit among all the people of God. We believe that the agreement we have here outlined is itself the product of a re-reception by Anglicans and Roman Catholic of doctrine about Mary and that it points to the possibility of further reconciliation, in which issues concerning doctrine and devotion to Mary need no longer be seen as communion-dividing . . .
>
> Paragraph 80

Anglican Archbishop Peter Carnley, former Primate of the Anglican Church of Australia and co-chairman of *ARCIC*, endorsed the work, and said "For Anglicans, the old complaint that these dogmas were not provable by scripture will disappear."

TIMELINE

1	Birth of Jesus Christ
33	Death of Jesus Christ
313	Emperor Constantine declares Christianity legal and builds Constantinople to be its center.
431	Oldest surviving break-away Christians, after Council of Ephesus, called variously Church of the East, Nestorian Church, Chaldean (today in union with Rome) and Assyrian, mainly in Iraq and Iran–550,000 adherents.
451	Second major surviving breakaway Christians, after the Council of Chalcedon. They do not recognize the Ecumenical Patriarch (of Constantinople) as a center of unity or the pope. 27 million members, mainly in Egypt, Ethiopia, and Syria
1054	Christianity breaks into East (Orthodox) and West (Roman Catholic).
1517	Martin Luther begins his public questioning of the Catholic Church.
1534	King Henry VIII breaks with Rome, and an English version of Roman Catholicism begins to emerge.
1545	Pope Paul III calls the Council of Trent, to reform the Catholic Church
1600 & 1700's	Many different Protestant churches are formed.
1789	United States Constitution enacted. The United States is the first country to form a government without an established religion, which was believed to be imprudent and risky. But the founders, while they believed in God, and most believed also in Jesus Christ, also believed that each human being deserved personal liberty of religious choice. Therefore, all religions (usually meaning different sects of Christianity) were equally worthy, except Roman Catholicism which was slightly suspicious because it had such a long history of establishment and power-sharing with monarchs.
1800's	Beginning of wide-spread disestablishment of church and state in Europe.
1868	The Anglican Communion takes shape at the first Lambeth Conference. It bring together bishops from around the world. Like the Roman Catholics, they focus on governance.
1870	In the face of modernity, the loss of papal lands, and a severe threat to papal existence, *Vatican I* declares the doctrine of infallibility.
1894	Abbe Portal, a French monk, and Lord Halifax, an Anglican nobleman, encourage their churches to discuss the doctrinal differences between Anglicans and Roman Catholics.
1896	In response to Portal and Halifax, the Vatican declares Anglican ordinations to be "absolutely null and utterly void."
1910	The ecumenical era begins with the first international meeting of the differing Christian denominations, at Edinburgh, Scotland.
1920	*The Appeal to all Christian People* issued at *Lambeth Conference*.
1921-25	*Malines Conversations* - first sanctioned and sustained ecumenical conversations between Rome and Canterbury.
1948	*World Council of Churches* is officially formed, and meets in Amsterdam, Holland.
1960	Archbishop of Canterbury Geoffrey Fisher visits Pope John XXIII at the Vatican, first visit by an English prelate to Rome since 1397

1962-65	*Vatican II* is called to explore new ways of thinking about Roman Catholic ecclesiology and its relationship to the modern world. Initiates outreach to other Christian denominations and to other religions.
1965	Pope Paul VI and Athenagoras, the Ecumenical Patriarch and leader of the Orthodox Church, meet and rescind the mutual excommunication decrees that had been in place for over 900 years, and initiate a dialogue.
1966	Archbishop of Canterbury Michael Ramsey, leader of the Anglican Communion, and Pope Paul VI sign the *Common Declaration* and begin a "serious dialogue which . . . may lead to that unity in truth for which Christ prayed."
1970	The *Anglican Roman Catholic International Commission* takes form and begins to meet annually, in order to explore and determine where there is and is not doctrinal agreement between the two churches. Nine agreed statements have been issued. The stated goal has been to seek full organic unity.
1974	Women are ordained in the Anglican Communion, in Philadelphia.
1995	Pope John Paul II issues the encyclical *Ut Unum Sint* which asks for help from all Christians, particularly theologians and pastors, in thinking about a form of papal primacy that is true to its essentials, but is open to a "new situation."
1999	The World Lutheran Federation and the Roman Catholic Church sign a *Common Declaration* stating essentially that Martin Luther's teaching that we are saved by God's freely given grace, and not by our good works, is correct.
2001	Bishops from the Roman Catholic and Anglican Churches are called to Mississauga, Canada to explore ways for the two churches to receive and make use of ARCIC's work.
2002	Rowan Williams elected 104th Archbishop of Canterbury
2003	The Episcopal Church in the USA approves the election of a practicing homosexual to be the bishop of New Hampshire, causing the unity of the Anglican Communion to come into question, thereby threatening all ecumenical progress.
2004	The Windsor Report comes out, recommending stronger bonds for the Anglican Communion, through a covenant process.
2005	John Paul II dies and Cardinal Joseph Ratzinger is elected pope, becoming Benedict XVI.
2005	Rome and Canterbury re-start IARCCUM, the group from Mississauga charged with getting ARCIC's agreed statements into the mainstream life of the churches.
2006	The Episcopal Church in the US elects Katharine Jefferts Schori as the new presiding bishop, the first female leader of one of the Anglican Communion's 38 provinces.
2006	The Church of England votes to allow the election of women to be bishops in England, though not until 2012.
2006	The Anglican Centre in Rome celebrates its 40th anniversary and Archbishop of Canterbury Rowan Williams officially visits Benedict XVI. They sign a Common Declaration that calls for greater study and reception, at the local level, of the agreed theological statements, and more working together in all possible areas.
2007	The Primates of the 38 provinces of the Anglican Communion meet in Tanzania, and contrary to predictions, Katharine Jefferts Schori is welcomed at the table. They issue a unanimous communiqué that asks the US House of Bishops to clarify their stated position on the blessing of same-sex unions and the approval of homosexual bishops, and bring it into line with official Communion teachings.

A HISTORY OF THE GREGORIAN CALENDAR

We take our calendar for granted, but it is actually an attempt to understand and to use complex astronomical facts to bring order to our social relationships. Historically, calendars have filled dual purposes: they of establish these systems for cultural as well as for religious purposes.

Today, the global household orders itself around the Gregorian calendar, which is set to the birth date of Jesus Christ. Why is this the case, and how did it come about?

Three important calendrical events are tied together here, and illustrate the evolution of the Gregorian calendar and also of its worldwide adoption.

In 46 BC, Julius Caesar, with help from an Egyptian astronomer named Sosigenes, made corrections to the existing calendar, which the Romans had inherited from the Babylonians. This new Julian calendar then spread widely because of the breadth of Roman Empire. It used the founding of Rome as year # 1. The term "ab urbe condite," (AUC) which means 'from the founding of the city,' refers to Rome. Under this calendar, Jesus Christ was born in 754 AUC.

In about 527, (or 1281 AUC) a Roman abbot and scholar, Dionysius Exiguus, decided that the birth of Jesus should become the new point from which to re-start the Julian calendar. He initiated the new term 'anni domini nostri Jesu Christi,' shortened to 'anno domini' (AD) and using the Julian calendar, he made the birth of Jesus Christ the year 1 AD. (Today, there is general agreement that his dates were not quite accurate.)

Over time, because of its inherent faults and the difficulties of measuring cosmic movement, the Julian calendar lost more and more of its accuracy. Finally, in 1582, Pope Gregory XIII initiated the needed calendar reforms by issuing the papal bull *Inter gravissimas*. The fundamental calendrical system, of days and months, stayed in place, but leap year was changed, and ten days were dropped from the calendar.

Renamed the Gregorian calendar, it took almost 350 years for it to be adopted worldwide. Most of Catholic Europe adopted it within a few years, but England waited until 1752. There is some irony in that it took the 1918 Russian Revolution to finally require Russian adoption of the pope's corrections.

As British subjects, the American Colonies adopted the Gregorian calendar when Britain did, in 1752. Wednesday, September 2, 1752 was followed by Thursday, September 14, 1752, since in the intervening years another day had been lost.

Another 'wrinkle in time' was the nonconforming first day of the year. From country to country, the first day of the year might be observed on January 1, March 1, March 25, or December 25.

> Previously in the colonies it was common for March 24 of one year to be followed by March 25 of the following year. This explains why, with the calendrical reform and the shift of New Year's Day from March 25 back to January 1, the year of George Washington's birth changed from 1731 to 1732. In the Julian calendar his birth date is February 11, 1731, but in the Gregorian calendar it is February 22, 1732.
>
> Peter Meyer

Today, the Gregorian calendar serves as the international standard for civil use, though even now, with all of our powerful scientific and computing powers, we are not able to perfectly calculate the movement of the celestial bodies. We don't even now precisely understand how the cosmos works.

It also demonstrates the embeddedness of Christianity in world consciousness and function. The separation between church and state has not filtered down to calendar use.

POPULATION BY CONTINENT

(400 BC to 1600 AD)

These totals demonstrate the density of population in Asia and Africa, as opposed to Europe, in the year 0.

YEAR	Asia	Europe	Russia	Africa	America	Oceania	World
400 BC	95	19	13	17	8	1	153
0	170	31	12	26	12	1	252
600	134	22	11	24	16	1	208
1000	152	30	13	39	18	1	253
1400	201	52	13	68	39	2	375
1500	245	67	17	87	42	3	461
1600	338	89	22	113	13	3	578

Source: J.N. Biraden, "Essai sur l'evolution du nombre des homes," Population 34 (1979)

Note: These are the numbers of one, among many, respected historical demographers. His numbers tend to represent a mid-range.

RESOURCES

> The Lund Principle: *"We should not do separately what we can do better or at least equally well together."*

The following resources have useful ideas for intra-Christian prayer and activity.

Flora Winfield
Growing Together, Working for Unity Locally, Society for Promoting Christian Knowledge, London, 2002

British Council of Churches
One Lord, One Faith, One Baptism, London, 1984
Guidelines and materials for interchurch worship

Pontifical Council Promoting Christian Unity
Directory for the Application of Principles and Norms on Ecumenism, Vatican City, 1993

Meyers, Ruth & Joanne M. Pierce, *God's Gift of Unity, A Study Guide for Episcopalians and Roman Catholics,* ARC/USA, 2004

There is an excellent Model Covenant among the churches in Papua New Guinea. It is easily available online and spells out ideas for local working together.

National Association of the Catechesis of the Good Shepherd
Bible-based spiritual formation for children ages 3 to 12. Highly admired and used equally by Anglican/Episcopalians and Roman Catholics

Cardinal Walter Kasper's new book, *A Handbook of Spiritual Ecumenism,* is full of ideas for prayer and spiritual activities, and starts from the premise that all Christians have things to learn from each other.

Growing Together in Unity and Mission, An Agreed Statement by the International Anglican – Roman Catholic Commission for Unity and Mission has two parts. The first explains achievements of ARCIC's theological dialogue. The second half is full of creative ideas for engaging in common mission and working toward the visible expression of their joint faith, including suggestions for preparing common material for use in preparing for baptism and confirmation, jointly renewing baptismal vows and even, where appropriate, using the same baptismal certificate. Both churches are also encouraged to pray for each other's leaders during weekly liturgies.

BIBLIOGRAPHY

Ahlstrom, S. E., *A Religious History of the American People*, Yale University Press, New Haven, CT, 1973

Anglican Consultative Council, *Called To Be One*, Morehouse Publishing, Harrisburg, PA, 1999

Appleby, R. Scott, *Church and Age Unite*, University of Notre Dame Press, Notre Dame, IN, 1992

Aveling et al, *Rome and The Anglicans*, W deGruyter, New York & Berlin, 1982

Avis, Paul, *Truth Beyond Words*, Cowley, Cambridge, MA, 1985

Barlow, Bernard, *A Brother Knocking At The Door*, The Canterbury Press, Norwich, England, 1996

Barrett David B. & Todd M. Johnson, *World Christian Trends AD 30 - AD 2200, Interpreting the Annual Christian Megacensus*, William Crey Library, Pasadena, CA, 2001

Baum, Gregory, *Ecumenical Theology Today*, Paulist Press, Glen Rock, NJ, 1964

Bea, Augustin, *The Unity of Christians*, Geoffrey Chapman, London, 1963

Bell, G. K. A., *Christian Unity: The Anglican Position*, Hodder and Stoughton Limited, London, 1948

Bell, G. K. A., *Randall Davidson, Archbishop of Canterbury*, Oxford, London, 1935

Bilaniuk, Petro B. T, *The Fifth Lateran Council (1512-1517) and the Eastern Churches*, Central Comm-Ukrainian Catholic Church, Toronto, 1975

Bird, David et al., *Receiving The Vision, The Anglican Roman Catholic Reality Today*, The Liturgical Press, Collegeville, MN, 1995

Bliss, Frederick M., *Catholic and Ecumenical, History and Hope, Why the Catholic Church is Ecumenical and What She is Doing About It*, Sheed & Ward, Franklin, WI, 1999

Brose, Olive J., *Frederick Dennison Maurice, Rebelious Conformist*, Ohio University Press, 1971

Buckley, Michael, *Papal Primacy and the Episcopate*, Crossroad, New York, 1998

Butler, David, *Dying To Be One, English Ecumenism: History, Theology and the Future*, SCM Press Ltd, London, 1996

Butler, Dom Cuthbert, *The Vatican Council 1869-70*, Newman Press, Westminster, MD, 1962

Campion, Edmund, ed., *Lord Acton and the First Vatican Council: A Journal*, Catholic Theological Faculty, Sydney, Australia, 1975

Cassidy, Cardinal Edward, *Ecumenism and Interreligious Dialogue*, Paulist Press, New York/Mahwah, 2005

Chadwick, Henry, *The Early Church*, Revised edition, Penguin Group, London, 1993

Chadwick, Owen, *A History of Christianity*, Phoenix Illustrated, London, 1997

Chadwick, Henry, ed., *Not Angels, But Anglicans, A History of Christianity in the British Isles*, The Canterbury Press, Norwich, England, 2000

Chapman, Dom John, *Studies on the Early Papacy*, Kennikat Press, Port Washington. NY & London, 1928

Clark and Davey, eds., *Anglican Roman Catholic Dialogue, Work of The Preparatory Committee*, Oxford University Press, New York, 1974

Coleman, Roger, ed., *Resolutions of the Twelve Lambeth Conferences, 1867-1988*, Anglican Book Centre, Toronto, 1992

Congar, Yves, *Tradition and Traditions*, Macmillan, New York, 1967

Curran, Charles, *Faithful Dissent*, Sheed & Ward, Kansas City, MO, 1986

Davie, Grace, *Religion in Modern Europe*, Oxford University Press, Oxford, 2000

Denaux, A (in collaboration with J Dick), *From Malines to ARCIC, The Malines Conversations Commemorated*, Leuven University Press, Leuven, Belgium, 1997

Dick, John A., *The Malines Conversations Revisited*, Leuven University Press, Leuven, Belgium, 1989

Duffy, Eamon, *Saints and Sinners, A History of the Popes*, Yale University Press, New Haven, CT, 1997

Dulles, Avery, *Resilient Church*, Doubleday, Garden City, NY, 1977

Dulles, Cardinal Avery, *Church Membership As A Catholic and Ecumenical Problem*, Marquette University, Theology Department, Milwaukee, 1974

Evans, G. R., *Method in Ecumenical Theology, The Lessons So Far*, Cambridge University Press, Cambridge, 1996

Evans, G. R., *Authority in the Church*, Canterbury Press, Norwich, UK, 1990

Falardeau, Ernest, *That All May Be One*, Paulist Press, New York, 2000

Fiedler, Maureen & Linda Rabben, eds., *Rome Has Spoken, A Guide to Frogotten Papal Statements*, Crossroad, New York, 1998

Fitzgerald, Penelope, *The Knox Brothers, Counterpoint*, Washington, DC, 2000

Franklin, William, et al, *Anglican Orders, Essays on the Centenary of Apostolicae Curae, 1896-1996*, Mowbray, London, 1996

Frend, W.H.C., *The Rise of Christianity*, Fortress Press, Philadelphia, 1984

Gibson, David, *The Coming Catholic Church, How The Faithful Are Shaping A New American Catholicism*, Harper San Francisco, San Francisco, CA, 2003

Gillis, Chester, *Roman Catholicism in America*, Columbia University Press, New York, 1999

Gillson, Etienne, *Wisdom and Love in St. Thomas Aquinas*, Marquette University Press, Milwaukee, 1951

Granfield, Patrick, *The Limits of the Papacy, Authority and Autonomy in the Church*, Crossroad, New York, 1987

Granfield, Patrick, The Papacy in Transition, Doubleday, New York, 1980

Greely, Andrew, *An Ugly Little Secret*, Sheed Andrews & McMeel, Kansas City, KS, 1977

Gros, Jeffrey, Rozanne Elder, Ellen K. Wondra, *Common Witness to the Gospel, Documents on Anglican-Roman Catholic Relations*, U. S. Catholic Conference, Washington, DC, 1997

Guillot, Laurentio B., *Ministry in Ecumenical Perspective, The Ministry of Priests and Priesthood As a Problem in Ecumenical Relations For Anglicans and Roman Catholics*, Catholic Book Agency, Rome, 1969

Haigh, Christopher, *English Reformations*, Oxford University Press, New York, 1993

Hale, Robert, *Canterbury and Rome, Sister Churches*, Paulist Press, New York, 1982

Harris, P. M. G., *Forms of Growth and Decline*, Praeger, Westport, CT, 2001

Hastings, Adrian, *The Theology of a Protestant Catholic*, SCM Press/ Trinity Press, London/Philadelphia, 1990

Hemmer, H., *Fernand Portal (1855-1926), Apostle of Unity* (trans. & ed. by Arthur T. Macmillan), Macmillan, London, 1961

Hill Christopher & E. J. Yarnold, *Anglicans and Roman Catholics, The Search for Unity*, SPCK/ICTS, London, 1994

Holmes, David L., *A Brief History of the Episcopal Church*, Trinity Press International, Valley Forge, PA, 1993

Hurley, Michael, *Christian Unity, An Ecumenical Second Spring*, Veritas, Dublin, 1999

Jasper, Ronald C. D., *George Bell, Bishop of Chichester*, Oxford University Press, London, 1967

Jinkins, Michael, *The Church Faces Death*, Oxford University Press, New York, 1999

Joyce, James, *A Portrait of the Artist As A Young Man*, Bantam Classic Book, New York, 1992

Kalilombe, Patrick & Mark Santer, *Unity From Below, Lessons from African Traditional Religion*, Selly Oaks Colleges, Birmingham, UK, 1993

Kasper, Cardinal Walter, *A Handbook of Spiritual Ecumenism*, New City Press, Hyde Park, NY, 2007

Kasper, Walter, *The Christian Understanding of Freedom and the History of Freedom in the Modern Era*, Marquette University Press, Milwaukee, WI, 1988

Kasper, Cardinal Walter, *That They All May Be One, The Call To Unity Today*, Burns & Oates, London, 2004

Kinnamon, Michael, *Why It Matters, A Popular Introduction to the Baptism, Eucharist & Ministry Text*, The World Council of Churches, Geneva, 1985

Kirvan, John J., ed., *The Infallibility Debate*, Paulist Press, New York, 1971

LaBarre, Weston, *The Ghost Dance*, Dell Publishing Company, New York, 1972

Leeming, Bernard, *The Vatican Councils and Christian Unity*, Darnton & Longmans, London, 1966

Legge, Alfred Owen, *The Growth of the Temporal Power of the Papacy*, Macmillan & Co, London, 1870

Lowell, C. Stanley, *The Ecumenical Mirage*, Baker Book House, Grand Rapids, MI, 1967

MacCulloch, Diarmaid, *Reformation, Europe's House Divided*, Allen Lane (Penguin Books), London, 2003

Mackie, J. D., *The Earlier Tudors 1485-1558*, Oxford University Press, 1952

Macquarrie, John, *Christian Unity and Diversity*, SCM Press, Ltd., London, 1975

Maurice, F. D., *The Kingdom of Christ*, J. M. Dent & Co., London, 1911

Maviiri, Ndidde, *Primacy in the Communion of Churches*, Pontificia Universitas Urbaniana, Rome, 1987

McAdoo, H. R., *Rome and The Anglicans*, W. deGruyter, Berlin, 1982

McClain, *Frank Mauldin Maurice, Man and Moralist*, SPCK, London, 1972

McCord, Peter, ed., *A Pope For All Christians*, Paulist, New York, 1976

McCoy, Alban, *An Intelligent Person's Guide to Catholicism*, Continuum, London, 2001

McGrath, Alister, *In The Beginning, The Story of the King James Bible*, Anchor Books, New York, 2001

Messenger, E. C., *Rome and Reunion*, Burns & Oates, London, 1934

Meyer, Harding & Lukas Vischer, eds., *Growth in Agreement*, Paulist Press/WCC, Ramsey, NJ, 1984

Minus, Paul M. Jr., *The Catholic Rediscovery of Protestantism*, Paulist Press, New York, 1976

Motter, Alton M., *Ecumenism 101, A Handbook About the Ecumenical Movement*, Forward Movement, Cincinnati, OH, 1997

Norman, E., *Roman Catholics in England*, Oxford University Press, New York, 1985

O'Collins, Gerald, *Living Vatican II, The 21st Council for the 21st Century*, Paulist Press, Mahwah, NJ, 2006

O'Collins, Gerald & Edward G. Farrugia, *A Concise Dictionary of Theology*, Paulist Press, Mahwah, NJ, 1991

O'Gara, Margaret, *The Ecumenical Gift Exchange*, Liturgical Press, Collegeville, MN, 1998

O'Grady, Desmond, *The Victory of the Cross*, Harper Collins Religious, London, 1992

Oppenheimer, Helen, *Marriage*, Mowbray, London, 1990

Parise, Michael, *Catholics and Ecumenism, That All May Be One*, Ligouri Publications, Ligouri, MO, 1989

Pawley, Bernard & Margaret, *Rome and Canterbury, Through Four Centuries*, Mowbrays, Oxford, 1971

Pawley, Bernard, *An Anglican View of the Vatican Council*, Greenwood Press, Westport, CT, 1973

Podmore, Colin, ed., *Community-Unity-Communion, Essays in Honour of Mary Tanner*, Church House Publishing, London, 1998

Porter, J. R., *Jesus Christ, The Jesus of History, The Christ of Faith*, Oxford University Press, NY/London, 1999

Porter, John F. & William J. Wolf, eds., *Toward The Recovery of Unity, The Thought of Frederick Dennison Maurice*, The Seabury Press, New York, 1964

Pottmeyer, Hermann, *Toward a Papacy in Communion, Perspectives from Vatican Councils I & II*, Crossroad, New York, 1998

Purcell, William, *Fisher of Lambeth*, Hodder & Stoughton, London, 1969

Purdy, William, *The Search For Unity*, Geoffrey Chapman, New York, 1996

Quinn, John R, *The Reform of the Papacy*, Crossroad, New York, 1999

Rahner, Karl, *The Shape of the Church To Come*, trans by Edward Quinn, The Seabury Press, New York, 1975

Ramsey, A. M., *The Gospel and the Catholic Church*, Longmans, Greens & Co., London, 1936

Randles, W. G. L., *The Unmaking of the Medieval Cosmos, 1500-1760*, Ashgate, Brookfield, VT, 1999

Ratzinger, Joseph Cardinal, *Salt of the Earth*, Interview/Peter Seewald, Trans./Adrian Walker, Ignatius Press, San Francisco, 1997

Ratzinger, Joseph Cardinal, *The Ratzinger Report*, Interview/Vittorio Messori, Ignatius Press, San Francisco, 1985

Ratzinger, Joseph Cardinal, *God and the World, A Conversation with Peter Seewald*, Ignatius Press, San Francisco, 2000

Reed, John Shelton, *Glorious Battle*, Vanderbilt University Press, Nashville, TN, 1996

Reese, Thomas, ed., *Episcopal Conferences*, Georgetown University Press, Washington, D.C., 1989

Reese, Thomas, *Inside The Vatican*, Harvard University Press, Cambridge, MA, 1996

Roberson, Ron, *The Eastern Christian Churches, A Brief Summary*, Orientalia Christiana, 6th Ed., Roma, 1999

Rogness, Michael, *The Church Nobody Knows, The Shaping of the Future Church*, Augsburg Publishing House, Minneapolis, MN, 1971

Rowland, Tracey, *Culture And The Thomist Tradition, After Vatican II*, Routledge, London, 2003

Rubenstein, Richard E., *Aristotles' Children, How Christians, Muslim and Jews Rediscovered Ancient Wisdom and Illuminated the Dark Ages*, Harcourt, New York, 2003

Ruthven, Malise, *Historical Atlas of the Islamic World*, Harvard University Press, Cambridge, MA, 2004

Rynne, Xavier, *John Paul's Extraordinary Synod*, Michael Glazier, Wilmington, DE, 1986

Sagovsky, Nicholas, *Ecumenism, Christian Origins and the Pracitce of Communion*, Cambridge University Press, Cambridge, UK, 2000

Santer, Mark, *Their Lord and Ours*, SPCK, London, 1982

Schatz, Klaus, *Papal Primacy, From Its Origins to the Present*, Liturgical Press, Collegeville, 1996

Schindler, David, ed., *Catholicism and Secularization in America, Our Sunday Visitor*, Huntington, IN, 1990

Schmidt, Stjepan, Augustin Bea, *The Cardinal of Unity* (trans. by Leslie Wearne), New City Press, 1992

Schreiter, Robert, *The New Catholicity*, Orbis Books, Maryknoll, NY, 1997

Schutz, Roger, *Unity, Man's Tomorrow*, Faith Press, London, 1962

Steinfels, Peter, *A People Adrift, The Crisis of the Roman Catholic Church in America*, Simon & Shuster, New York, 2003

Stott, John, *Evangelical Anglicans and the ARCIC Final Report*, Church of England Evangelical Council, London, 1982

Sykes, Stephen W., ed., *Authority in the Anglican Communion*, Anglican Book Centre, Ontario, 1987

Sykes, Stephen W., et al, *The Study of Anglicanism*, SPCK/Fortress, London, NY, 1999

Tanner, Norman P., *The Councils of the Church, A Short History*, Crossroad Publishing Company, New York, 2001

Tanner, Mary, *One In Christ*, Volume 39, No 1, January, 2004

Tavard, George H., *The Quest for Catholicity, A Study in Anglicanism*, Herder & Herder, New York, 1964

Tavard, George H., *Two Centuries of Ecumenism*, Burns & Oates, London, 1961

Tavard, George H., *The Church, Community of Salvation, An Ecumenical Theology*, The Liturgical Press, "Collegeville, MN", 1992

Temple, William, *Thoughts on Some Problems of the Day*, Macmillan & Co, London, 1931

Tierney, Brian, *Origins of Papal Infallibility 1150-1350*, E. J. Brill, Leiden, 1972

Tillard, Jean-Marie, *I Believe, Despite Everything*, Translated by William D. Rusch, Liturgical Press, Collegeville, MN, 2000

Tracy, James D., *Europe's Reformations 1450-1650*, Rowman & Littlefield, Lanham, Maryland, 1999

Tracy, David, *On Naming The Present, Reflections on God, Hermenuetics and Church*, Orbis Books, New York, 1994

Turner, Timothy J., *Welcoming The Baptized*, Grove Books, New York, 1996

Turner, Frank M., *John Henry Newman, The Challenge of Evangelical Religion*, Yale University Press, New Haven, CT, 2002

Van Dyck, Maria J., *Growing Closer Together, Rome And Canterbury: A Relationship of Hope*, St. Paul Publications, UK, 1992

Visser 't Hooft, W. A. , *Anglo-Catholicism and Orthodoxy, A Protestant View*, SCM Press, London, 1933

von Arx, Jeffrey, ed., *Varieties of Ultramontanes*, Catholic University of America Press, Washington, DC, 1998 von Balthazar, Hans Urs, *A Short Primer for Unsettled Laymen*, Ignatius Press, San Francisco, CA, 1987

Wagemaker, Matthieu, *Two Trains Running, The Rception of the Understanding of Authority*, Peter Lang, Bern, 1999

Ware, Timothy, *The Orthodox Church*, Penguin, New York, 1997

Weigel, George, *Catholic Theology in Dialogue*

Weigel, George, *Witness To Hope*, Cliff Street Books, New York, 1999

Williams, Rowan, *Lost Icons*, T&T Clark, Edinburgh, 2000

Witmer, J. W. & J. R.Wright, *Called To Full Unity, Documents on Anglican*, US Catholic Conference, Washington, DC, 1986

Woloch, Isser, *18th Century Europe, Tradition and Progress 1715-1890*, W W Norton, New York, 1982

Wright, J. Robert, ed., *A Communion of Communions, One Eucharistic Fellowship*, Seabury Press, New York, 1979

Wright, J. Robert & Herbert J. Ryan, *Episcopalians and Catholics, Can They Ever Get It Together?*, Dimension Books, Denville, NJ, 1972

Yarnold, E. J. & Henry Chadwick, *An ARCIC Catechism, Questions and Answers on the Final Report*, Catholic Truth Society, London, 1983

Dictionary of the Ecumenical Movement, WCC Publications, Geneva, 2002

Rule of St. Benedict, Liturgical Press, Collegeville, MN, 2000

ACKNOWLEDGEMENTS

This has turned out to be a much longer project than I thought it would be, but I've loved every (almost) minute of it. I've gotten superior advice and kind support at each step.

I dedicate this book to my parents, Betty and Jim Sorensen, and to my siblings – Fran Taylor, Stephanie Fredericks, Drew Sorensen, and Sally Howard. The heart and soul of its ideas were formed around the kitchen table of our childhood. They mean the world to me.

For my husband Henry and our daughter Frances – who some how understood why this was so important to me and why I spent so much time in the sub-basement of Firestone Library at Princeton University.

To Holly Ketron, who was always willing to help me to think and write more clearly.

I want to especially thank two people who, midway through, carefully read the ms and offered extensive and substantive comments – Mary Tanner, a former Anglican member of the Anglican Roman Catholic International Commission and currently the European President of the World Council of Churches, and Father Don Bolen, a staff officer at the Pontifical Council for Promoting Christian Unity and the Co-Secretary of the Anglican Roman Catholic International Commission. Their encouragement gave me the confidence to keep plugging away. William G. Rusch, George Tavard, Gerald O'Collins, Stephen Platten, and Robert Jenson also read it closely and saved me from a number of "howlers."

For the theologians and ecumenists who open-heartedly listened, advised and, in some cases, read the book in manuscript – Frank Griswold, J. Robert Wright, Louis Weil, Bill Franklin, David Reed, Gerald O'Collins, Donald Gerardi, John Flack, Stephen Platten, Phoebe Pettingell, John Baycroft, Vivian and Bruce Ruddock, Mary Donovan, Ian Douglas, Steven Charleston, and to the members of the Boston Theological Consortium who helped me, at the very beginning, to think about what I was trying to do.

Thanks to Karin Trainer, Sam Hynes and Mary Cross who gave me quiet places to work.

For librarians Steve Kueler, at the Episcopal Divinity School/Weston Library, Cheryl Adams at the Library of Congress, Kate Skrebutenas at Princeton Theological Seminary, and Wayne Blivens-Tatum at Princeton University.

For friends and acquaintances who took an interest and offered support over the last nine years: Warren Ilchman, Sam Vaughan, Bettina Milliken and David Padwa, Michelle Preston, Philip Howard, Ivan Head, Charlie and Caroline Persell, Mary Moore Gaines, John McPhee, Kemp Battle, Norman and Zulie

Catir, Mary Rower, John Andrew, Sally Arteseros, Susannah Agnelli, Gugu Ortona, Ledlie and Roxana Laughlin, Virginia Reath, Margery Cuyler and Jan Perkins, Bo Polk, Bruce Bayne, Margaret Pawley and helpful others.

For Ross Miller and Jed Lyons at Rowman & Littlefield, and very especially to Jerry Kelly, designer and friend.

Lastly, to the glory of libraries and those who work in them – each person in that quiet, trying to make some sense out of the clanging disorder and competing ideas of all those different books.